THE
COMPLEAT
PARISH OFFICER

Published by
WILTSHIRE FAMILY HISTORY SOCIETY

Published by Wiltshire Family History Society

10 Castle Lane, Devizes, Wilts, SN10 1HU

Registered Charity No. 290284

Seventh Edition 1734

Facsimile edition 1990

New Edition 1996

ISBN 1 898714 21 5

Edited and typeset by Rosemary Church

Our thanks to John Lywood for proof reading and supplying
the list of references.

FOREWORD

This little book was part of the library of my husband, Edwyn Charles Birchenough M.A. (Oxon) 1911-1969. He said he had bought it for sixpence off a barrow in Leather Lane market; that would have been about 1933 when he was in London studying for a post-graduate Diploma at London University Institute of Education.

His main interest was the Primer in English, (the beginnings of our Book of Common Prayer). He established a considerable reputation in that field but, in addition, he was highly suspicious of the accuracy of the then received view of social and economic history of the 16th, 17th and 18th centuries, a view that is rapidly being changed by modern family historians.

The Compleat Parish Officer is a handbook for those who had to apply and interpret the increasingly complex laws enacted to deal with the various social problems as they arose, its starting point being the Great Poor Law Act of 1601 and its various amendments. This edition, published in 1734, brings it up to date.

The wording of the Act, under which action can be taken, is quoted *in extenso* giving chapter and verse and, where appropriate, cases are quoted in interpretation. I understand that the general approach and format are still in use today, in handbooks used by the Police and modern magistrates.

I hope the handbook will be equally useful to today's family historians as they delve into the 'parish chest' material after the ancestor who was the Surveyor of the Highways, or who had become entangled with the laws about Settlement.

I wish to thank the Publications Sub-Committee of N.W.Kent Family History Society for being prepared to accept this little book for re-publication, also Mrs. Jean A. Cole of *Family Tree* magazine for her enthusiastic support for the idea of re-publication, and to Dartford Public Library for enabling me to take the original photocopies on their excellent machine.

Josephine Birchenough

JOSEPHINE BIRCHENOUGH nee Redhead (1920 - 1994)

Josephine Birchenough was a remarkable lady. A woman of many parts: deeply involved in local and family history, speaking French and excellent Polish, her smattering of Mandarin and Russian reflecting her travels in advanced years, travels that included visiting her birthplace Australia. Josephine could sew, knit and embroider; sang in the Blackheath Choir, served in the army and worked in chemicals, was a Butlins Redcoat, followed many sports, and taught keep fit to the elderly. She was caring and thoughtful, giving generously of herself to anyone who needed her help. Josephine made an indelible impression on everyone. She could "walk with kings - nor lose the common touch". With husband, Edwyn, she worked on archaeological digs and made an exhaustive study of Lee in Kent to become the expert on Lee history, her notes and indexes carefully preserved. Widowed early, with two young children, she was forced to earn her living. She cared deeply for her family (and her cat Sooty) supporting each one when needed. Documentation of her families, some parts of the story written up, has been preserved for posterity.

A founder member of this Society, Josephine immediately volunteered to help, writing copiously for the Journal and regularly recording monumental inscriptions. On the Publications Committee she was invaluable, particularly in preparation of West Kent Sources, working prodigiously for the forthcoming publication on schools' records. Any Society activity involved Josephine in some capacity, described by a long-standing friend and member as "a jolly good soldier". Later, with the Society Committee, setting up Dartford Branch, chairing and training a group of willing volunteers new to family history and committee work. The Branch still bears her mark.

By chance she learned and perfected a new skill, typsetting, one that enhanced our Journal (and others) for several years. "I did a little sub-editing" she would say, meaning corrected an error or added a relevant point or two, relishing her part in producing our Journal and in its high reputation. It is fitting that Josephine had been made an honorary member of the Society.

The energy of the woman, even in latter years, was remarkable, adding to her activities work such as indexing WO 97 army records for the Public Record Office project and taking groups to main repositories. So many will benefit in future from her work without ever knowing her; that would have pleased her. With considerable pride she accepted The Institute for Historical Research's honour for her work in local history and, at 70, was particularly happy at passing examinations for Licentiate of the Institute of Heraldic & Genealogical Studies.

Josephine could be exasperating (her words) whether determined to do things her own way or by refusing to curtail her activities after four serious throat operations, despite her 70 years. It was equally typical to have drafted notes for the student nurses on treating voiceless patients. Generally philosophical, sustained by a strong Christian faith, Josephine was so independent but always genuinely grateful for help from others; always true to her own beliefs, fiercely defending whatever she felt to be right.

A real character, eccentric, Josephine arrived on her motor bike for most events until she was 70, a matronly figure in bright yellow waterproofs "her crash helmet framing those rosy cheeks", all removed to reveal her "Hell's Granny" T shirt, reflecting her modern and optimistic outlook. It has also been known for her to take over from the guide in a museum. As an adult education tutor of family history Josephine "taught with such a great sense of humour and enthusiasm" inspiring students, recruiting members. She was a performer; it was the way she put over 'teaching points' (her words). Who could forget Josephine mimicking a lion rampant. She delighted in seeing fledgling family historians grow in confidence and expertise in their quest for ancestors. We shall remember Josephine for "her memory over a casual remark", producing pertinent references within days. As friend, colleague or member we shall miss "this wonderful lady", Josephine with her "love of life", miss seeing her living it to the full

NWK FHS Journal Volume 6 No. 10, July 1994.

THE COMPLEAT PARISH OFFICER containing

I. The Authority and Proceedings of High Constables, Petty Constables, Headboroughs, and Tithingmen, in every Branch of their Duties, pursuant to Acts of Parliament: With the High Constables Precepts, Presentments, Warrants *etc.*

II. Of Churchwardens, how chosen, their Business in Repairing of Churches, Bells, *etc.* and Assigning of Seats; the Manner of Passing their Accounts, and the Laws concerning the Church in all Cases; and an Abstract of the Act for building Fifty new Churches in *London* and *Westminster*. Also of Sidesmen, and their Duty; and Vestrymen, *etc.*

III. Of Overseers of the Poor, and their Office; their Power in Relieving, Employing and Settling, *etc.* of poor Persons; the Laws relating to the Poor, and Settlements, and the Statutes concerning Masters and Servants.

IV. Of Surveyors of the Highways, and Scavengers, how elected, their Business in amending the Ways, *etc.* and the Duty of others, with the Methods of Taxation, and Laws of the Highways.

Together with the STATUTES relating to Hackney Coaches and Chairs, *etc.*

The Seventh Edition corrected, with very large ADDITIONS.

To which is added the Office of Constables, written by Sir *FRANCIS BACON*, Knt. in the Year 1610, declaring what Power they have, and how they ought to be cherished in their Office.

In the SAVOY:

---- by E. and R. NUTT, and R. GOSLING, ----- of Edw. Sayer, Esq;) for Bernard ---- *Temple-Bar*, and H. Birt, at the ---- *Mary-Lanes* M DCC XXXIV.

THE PREFACE.

The very great Deficiency in the Books hitherto published of this Nature, with Relation to the Business of Church-wardens and Overseers of the Poor, will be a sufficient Apology for my Engaging in this Undertaking; There being no Treatise yet extant, that contains any tolerable Directions for Dispatch of the Business and Variety of Proceedings, incident to those extensive Offices, especially in this populous City.

The other Books on this Subject, are likewise very defective in the Office of Constables; I having, besides at least twenty intire new Heads, made very Considerable Additions and Improvements to what has hitherto appeared, with respect to them: And the Business of Surveyors of the Highways, is no less neglected by other Authors; so that I have sufficient Room to introduce this small Performance.

I have taken Care that no particular Thing of any Signification, relating either to Constables, Church-wardens, Overseers of the Poor, or Surveyors of the Highways, is wanting in this new Edition to render it compleat; and as a farther Recommendation, I think it incumbent on me to signify that I have thoroughly examined my References, and compared my Book with the Articles referr'd to, whereby the Plebean, unacquainted with our Laws and Statutes, may be assured of his acting with Safety, without advising with other Persons, or consulting any Authority but the Treatise.

This I doubt not will be a Satisfaction to Parish-Officers, to have so many valuable Informations communicated in so small a Compass. By the Means the Purchase is in every one's Power, so that nothing might be omitted, which may be a tribute to the Usefulness of this Tract, I have inserted an Abstract of the Statutes for building fifty new Churches in London and Westminster, several Magnificent Structures being now erected pursuant to those Laws; and I conclude, next to treating of Carmen, (under the Head Scavengers) with the Statutes concerning Hackney Coaches, and Chairs and Watermen, etc.

N.B. In a large Octavo Volume, called Parish Law, lately published, the Author under most of the general Titles, hath notoriously transcribed the Pages verbatim from me, but sometimes with great and very material Omissions; and where-ever he has departed from my Guide, he is in the greatest? Wilderness, and hath frequently the same, Then over and over again, at least three or four Times to swell and add to the Price of his extraordinary Treatise.

G.

THE Compleat Parish-Officer.

OF CONSTABLES.

High and Petty Constables, Headboroughs, and Tithingmen; and their Authority.

The Office of a Constable is of great Antiquity, and both High and Petty Constables are Officers at Common Law: One was appointed long before the Statute of *Winton*, (some Writers tell us, in the Reign of King *Alfred*, on the Division of Counties into Hundreds, for the Ease of the Sheriff) and the other before the Reign of King *Edward* III.

Before Justices of the Peace were made, Constables were Conservators of the Peace; they might put a Man in the Stocks who broke the Peace, might arrest or imprison one for beating or maiming another, and had several other Powers and Privileges; but they could not take Security by Recognizance or Bail, because they were not Officers on Record. *Owen 105.* And some of our Law Books mention, that Constables were only subordinate Officers to the Conservators of the Peace, as they are now to the Justices.

The Statute of *Winchester, 13 Ed.1.* hath appointed two High Constables in every Hundred; and Continuance of Time, and Increase of People and Offences, have made Petty Constables necessary in Towns and Parishes, as Assistants to the High Constables; and there are Headboroughs, Tithingmen, *etc.* for particular Boroughs, Hamlets, Tithings and Villages.

The Petty Constables and Tithingmen are not subordinate to the High Constable in any Thing that proceeds from his own Authority merely, though his Power is of a larger Extent than theirs; and in Places where there are no Constables, but Tithingmen, *etc.*, there the Authority of such Parish-Officer equals that of the Constable, within his Limits; for he is in Effect the Constable of the Place.

But Headboroughs, Tithingmen, *etc.* appointed in a Town or Parish, having also a Constable, cannot principally concern themselves in any Matter, the Constables being Head Officers; though in the Absence of the Constable, they are chiefly to attend the Service; And there are many Things which a Constable has Power to do, that Headboroughs and Tithingmen cannot intermeddle with. *Dalt.3.*

High Constables are chosen either at the Quarter-Sessions, or in the Court Leet; and where the Latter is warranted by Custom, the Justices of Peace cannot interpose, unless it be on a Neglect of keeping such Court, or in chusing them, when the Justices at their Quarter-Sessions may appoint and swear a High Constable, or issue their Warrant to do it out of the Sessions; but in Case of Refusal to serve the Office, Death, or Removal, a Justice of Peace may chuse and swear another, tho' this is generally done by two Justices; and the Person chosen is to continue in the Office till the next Court Leet, or the Sessions, and then the Steward or Justices may either approve him, or appoint another, to continue in for one Year.

If he is present when chosen, and refuses to take upon him the Office, the Steward may fine him; (Justices of Peace may likewise bind him over to the Assizes, or Sessions, where he may be indicted, and fined.) If he does not appear, the Homage are to present his Refusal at the next Court, whereupon he shall be amerced; and if he being present accept the Office, he is to be forthwith sworn in the Leet. If absent, upon Notice given by the Steward, he is to take the Oath before the Leet. If absent, upon Notice given by the Steward, he is to take the Oath before a Justice. *Dalt.58, etc.*

Petty Constables and Tithingmen are elected by the Parish, and sworn in their Offices in the Court-Leet, and sometimes by Justices of Peace in the Sessions: And the Sessions may remove High Constables and Petty Constables, the Justices there being the best Judges in these Cases. *1 Salk.150.*

Dissenters chosen Constables, are to make Deputies for the Execution of the Office. *1 W. & M.* And other Persons may make Deputies, though formerly it was doubted; but they must answer for their Miscarriages, unless such Deputies are sworn and allowed by the Court. *Sid.355.* And if the Office happen on a Woman, where there is a Custom for every Inhabitant to serve by Turns, she may hire one to execute the Office. *Sid.355.*

As for Persons qualified for this Office, they ought to be honest, understanding, and able Men; to be Men of Substance, and not of the meaner Sort; wherefore they are not to be elected by House, or Custom, if not fit to execute the Office: They are likewise to be resident where chosen; and if they are not thus qualified, upon Complaint, two Justices may appoint others.

Justices of the Peace, Clergymen, Attornies, Lawyers, Physicians, Ideots, Poor, Old and Sick Persons, are exempted from serving.

When Constables are appointed, the Steward of the Court-Leet, or the Justices, administer the following Oath.

Oath of Constables.

You shall well and truly serve our Sovereign Lord the King, and the Lord of this Leet, (if appointed in the Court-Leet) in the Office of a Constable, in and for the Hundred of A. or Parish of, etc. until you be thereof discharged, according to due Course of Law, or for the Year ensuing, and until another shall be sworn in your Room; you shall from Time to Time well and truly do and execute all Things belonging to the said Office, according to the best of your Knowledge. So help you God.

Note; The Oaths of Allegiance and Supremacy, appointed by Stat. *25 Car.2* do not extend to Constables, Church-wardens, *etc.*

Formerly Constables were sworn to several Articles, *viz.* To suppress and present Affrays; arrest armed Men; present Bloodshed and Drunkenness; apprehend Felons; present Gaming houses and Gamesters; make Hue and Cry; punish idle Persons, Nightwalkers, *etc.*; present Rescues; apprehend Rioters; punish Vagabonds; execute Warrants; keep Watch, *etc.*

These are to be enquired into by all Constables; and the Duty of a High Constable alone consists in the following Articles.

Duty of High Constables alone.

The High Constable, when established in his Office, has the Direction of the Petty Constables, Headboroughs and Tithingmen, within the Hundred. His Duty in general is to keep the Peace, and apprehend Felons, Rioters, *etc.* to make Hue and Cry after Felons; and take Care that the Watch be duly kept in the Hundred, and that the Statutes for punishing Rogues and Vagrants be put in Execution. He ought to present unlawful Gaming, Tippling and Drunkenness, Bloodshed, Affrays, *etc.*

To return all Victuallers and Alehouse-keepers that are unlicensed, and such Persons as entertain Inmates; he is to present Bakers who sell Bread under Weight; Brewers selling Beer to unlicensed Alehouses; Forestallers, Ingroffers, *etc. Dalt. c.28.*

He must likewise present the Defaults of Petty Constables, Headboroughs, *etc.* who neglect to apprehend Rogues, Vagabonds and idle Persons, Whores, Night-Walkers, *etc.* and also all Defects of Highways and Bridges, and the Names of those who ought to repair them; Scavengers that neglect their Duty, and all common Nuisances: And he is to execute Precepts and Warrants directed to him by Justices of Peace; and make Returns to the Sessions of the Justices, to all the Articles concerning his Office. *Lamb.125; Stat. 12 Ann.*

The High Constable may determine Complaints of Clothiers and their Spinners, and other Labourers; by Virtue of an old Statute relating to not paying Wages in ready Money, *etc.* which incurs a Forfeiture of three Times the Value of the Wages: And on Non payment of the Forfeitures, *etc.* may commit the Party 'till paid. *Stat. 4 Ed.4. c.1.*

A High Constable may enter into any Place to search for Tenters, Ropes, *etc.* for stretching of Cloth; and if he finds any, he is to deface them; and if the Owners shall afterwards make use of them, such High Constable has Power to seize and sell them, and distribute the Money to the Poor. *Stat. 39 Eliz. c.20.* Persons resisting the Constable, forfeit £10.

High Constables on their receiving Monies from Church-wardens assessed on any Parish for Relief of poor Prisoners, are to pay over the same to the Collectors appointed by the Justices at the Quarter Sessions, on the Penalty of £5. *Stat. 14 Eliz. c.5.*

They are also to pay over Monies received for the Relief of Prisoners in the *King's Bench* and *Marshalsea*, under the Penalty of 20s. And so of Money received for the Relief of maimed Soldiers and Mariners, on Pain of 40s. *Stat. 43 Eliz. c.3.*

High Constables are likewise to pay Monies raised at *Easter*-Sessions, for the Use of the Poor, to the Treasurers, under the Penalty of 20s. *Stat. 43 Eliz. c.2.*

Chief Constables are to pay Petty Constables the Allowances ascertained in Certificates made by Justices for passing of Vagrants, and no more, taking the Certificates and their Receipts; which Certificates and Receipts are to be allowed the Chief Constable in his Account by the Treasurer of the County. *Stat. 12 Ann. c.23.*

High Constables paying Money for passing of Vagrants, without the Petty Constables producing a Receipt for such Vagrants, to forfeit 20s. *Stat. 1 Ann Sess.2. c.13.*

High Constables are to issue Precepts to Petty Constables, to prepare Lists of Jurors; to make Presentments of Offences; and levy Gaol-Money, *etc.*

Constables of London.

There being some Variation in the Manner of Election, and the Oath and Office of Constables in the City of *London*, with respect to other Constables appointed in the Country; I shall here communicate some Observations relating to them, before I proceed to the particular Business and Power of Constables.

The Compleat Parish Officer - Constables.

And first the City is divided into 26 Wards, and every Ward into the like Number of Precincts, over each of which is a proper Constable.

All Constables ought to be Freemen of the City: They are nominated by the Inhabitants of the Precinct on St. *Thomas's* Day, and confirm'd, or otherwise at the Court of Wardmote; and after they are confirm'd, they are Sworn in their Offices at a Court of Aldermen, on the next *Monday* after *Twelfth-Day. Calthr. Rep. p.129.*

The Substance of the *Oath* is as follows; To keep the King's Peace to the utmost of their Power; to arrest Affrayers, Rioters, and such as make Contests to the Breach of the Peace, and to lead them to the House of Correction, or Compter of one of the Sheriffs; and in Case of Resistance, to make Outcry on them, and pursue them from Street to Street, and from Ward to Ward, till they are arrested.

To search for common Nusances in their respective Wards; (being required by Scavengers, *etc.*) and upon Request to assist the Beadle and Raker in collecting their Salaries and Quarterage; to present to the Mayor and Ministers of the City, Defaults relating to the Ordinances of the City; to certify in the Mayor's Court, once a Month, the Names and Surnames of all Freemen deceas'd; and also of the Children of such Freemen, being Orphans.

And by the Articles of the Wardmote Inquest, Constables are to certify the Name, Surname, Place of Dwelling, Profession and Trade of every Person, who shall newly come to inhabit in their Precincts, and to keep a Roll thereof: In Order to this, they are to make Enquiry, at least once a Month, into what Persons are lately come to lodge and sojourn there: And if they find by their own Concessions, or the Records of the Aldermens Books, that such new Comers are ejected from any other Ward for bad Living, or any Misdemeanour, and refuse to find Sureties for their Good Behaviour, Warning is to be given to them and their Landlords, that they depart; and on Refusal, they may be imprison'd, and their Landlords fined a Year's Rent, agreed for by such new Comers. *Calth. Rep. 138.*

Constables in each Ward are to attend the Watch by Turns, one every Night, and to go the Rounds; and with the Beadles every Night are to warn such Persons as are to serve upon the Watch in their several Precincts; and if they refuse to appear, the Constable may hire others in their Stead, and they shall pay the Constable, according to the Custom of the City. The Common Council appoint the Watchmen.

They are to certify to the Lord Mayor and Common Council of the City, the Names of such Persons as shall interrupt or hinder them in the Discharge of their Offices.

These are the Articles of the Oath, and extraordinary Business of the Constables of *London*; to which I am to add, that a Constable of *London* has Power to execute Warrants, *etc.* throughout the whole City, upon Occasion: And such as are chosen into the Office are obliged to place the King's Arms, and the Arms of the City, over their Doors; and if they reside in Alleys, at the End of such Alleys, towards the Street, to signify that a Constable lives there, and that they may be the more easily found when wanted.

I come now to *Constables at large.*

The Duty and Authority in general of Constables in their several Towns, Parishes, *etc.* is much the same as the High Constable hath in his Hundred: They are to keep the Peace, and may break into a House to see the Peace kept; make fresh Pursuit into another County, *etc.* They may also command all Persons to assist them, and take into Custody any whom they see committing a Felony, or breaking of the Peace; but a Constable cannot detain a Man at his Pleasure, only stay him to bring him before some Justice, to be examined and committed, *etc. Dalt. c.1. 8. H.P.C. 93, 135.*

Part of their Office consists in Attendance on Justices of Peace, at Courts-Leet, and on Coroners for executing of Warrants; they are likewise to attend upon Judges of Assize at the Gaol-delivery, Justices at the General and Special Sessions, and other Meetings, to execute Warrants; and present Offences upon Oath, according to Articles exhibited, *etc.*

Their Duty in particular is to be considered under the several Heads following, *etc.* Affrays, Alehouses, Arms, Arrests, Artificers, Bakers, Bastardy, Bawdy-Houses, Bridges, Butter, Buttons, Carriages, Cattle, Clothiers, Coals, Conventicles, Customs, Deer-stealing, Deserters, Distillers, Distress, Drunkenness, Dyers, Escapes, Excise, Felons, Fish, Forcible Entry, Foreign Goods, Forestallers, Game, Gaming, Gaol and Gaolers, Gunpowder, Hawkers, Hay-Market, Hedge-breakers, Highways, Horses, Hue and Cry, Inns, Juries, Labourers, Land-Tax, Maltsters, Measures, Militia, Night walkers, Orchards robbed, Physicians, Plague, Popish Recusants, Post-Letters, Presentments, Prisons, Prisoners, Riots, Rogues, Robbery, Sabbath, Servants, Shoemakers, Soldiers, *Supersedeas*, Swearing, Taylors, Tithes, Tobacco, Vagrants, Watch, Warrants, Weights, Wrecks, *etc.* And first, the Authority of Constables in Affrays.

Affrays.

Affray is a Fighting between two or more; and there must be a Stroke given, or a Weapon drawn.

A Constable may command Affrayers to depart on Pain of Imprisonment; and if they refuse, or make Resistance, he may justify the Beating of them, and call others to his Assistance. *Dalt.35.; 4 Co. 4.*

Affrayers not ceasing, but still threatning to wound each other, he may put in the Stocks 'till he can carry them before a Justice; or if any Assault be made upon the Constable, he may not only defend himself, but put the Parties in the Stocks, as aforesaid, 'till he can convey them before a Justice, or to the Gaol. *Dalt. s. 4, 5, 35, etc. Kitch 69.* And if a Constable, or his Assistants, shall happen to be killed, it is Murder; and if they are wounded in the Affray, they shall have good Damages; but the Affrayers in such Case shall be without Remedy. *Lamb.141, 142.*

If any Person shall assault, threaten to kill or beat another in the Presence of a Constable, or do any other Act which amounts to a Breach of the Peace, the Constable has Power to carry the Offender before a Justice without Warrant; but if the Affray or Breach of the Peace is over before he comes, he may not arrest the Affrayers without a Justice's Warrant, except some Person be dangerously hurt. And if there be nothing but Words, the Constable may not lay Hands on them. *Dalt.36.; 38 H.8. c.6.*

If a Person be desperately wounded in an Affray, the Constable may arrest the Offender, and carry him before a Justice, who is either to bail or commit him, until it be known whether the Party will live or die. *4 Co.4; 9 Co.66; Lamb.135*. Any Person may arrest Affrayers, where there is a dangerous Affray, and deliver them to the Constable. *Dalt.35.*

A Constable may pursue Affrayers into any other Franchise or County; but out of the County he is only an Assistant to the Constables there; and he may justify the Breaking open Doors to apprehend Affrayers, and keep the Peace. *Plow.37.; Cromp.146.; Lamb. 135, 185, etc.*

All this the Constable may do *ex Officio*, without Commandment or Precept from a Justice, except as above, where an Affray is over before he has Notice; and it has been held, that the Constables might *ex Officio* take Sureties for the Peace. *Trin. 35 Eliz. Skarret's* Case: But it was then the Opinion of others, that he ought to carry the Offender before a Justice; and our ancient Books tell us, that a Constable may not, at the Request of any Person, take Surety of the Peace, though he is to do what lies in his Power to keep the Peace. *3 Hen.4, cap. 9.; Kitchen 62.; Cromp.6, etc.*

If Persons make an Affray, and the Constable refuses to go to keep the Peace, being informed of it, he may be fined in the Sessions, on Presentment by the Grand Jury. *Cromp.846.*

Alehouses.

What I shall mention under this Head, is the Punishment for Neglects of Constables.

If a Constable do not levy the Penalty of 20s. by Distress for the Poor, inflicted on Persons keeping Alehouses without Licence; or if there be no Distress, he neglects to whip the Offender, he is liable to a Forfeiture of 40s. or to Commitment until the Alehouse keeper is punished. *Stat. 1. Jac.1. c.9.; Car.1. c.4.*

Not delivering the Poor's Moiety of the Penalty of 6s. 8d. *per* Barrel, for selling Ale to an unlicensed Alehouse keeper, over to the Church-wardens, *etc.* and they not distributing it among the Poor, forfeit double the Value. *Stat. 4 Jac.1. cap.4.*

And not levying 20s. on Alehouse-keepers for selling less than Measure, he forfeits 40s. to the Use of the Poor, to be levied by Distress; and if no Distress, to be committed. Selling in unmarked Vessels, *etc.* incurs a Forfeiture not above 40s. nor under 10s. one Moiety to the Informer, the other to the Poor. *11 & 12 W.*

Not levying 10s. on Alehouse Keepers for suffering Persons to sit tippling, to forfeit *ut supra. Stat. 1 Jac.1.; 21 Jac.1. c.7.*

Also not levying 3s. 4d. on Persons convicted of Tippling, forfeits 10s. But in all these Cases, there must be a Justice's Warrant.

A Duty is granted by a late Act to be paid yearly by Alehouse-keepers in *London* and *Westminster*, leviable by Commissioners; who are to grant Permissions for Retailing Beer or Ale, the not taking out whereof incurs a Penalty of £20 *etc. Stat. 12 Geo.1. c.12.*

Distillers selling Brandy by Retail to be Licensed as common Alehouse-Keepers, by *Stat. 2 Geo.2. c.28.*

Arms.

Constables may stop all such Persons as go or ride unlawfully armed in Terror of the People; take away their Arms, and carry them before a Justice of the Peace, to find Sureties of the Peace. *2 Ed.3 .c.3.; 7 R.2.; Dalt.35.*

His Majesty's Servants or Officers, Persons pursuing Hue and Cry in Case of Felony, and other Offences, have lawful Authority to bear Armour or Weapons. *Dalt.c.9. fol. 36.; 3 Co. Inst.162.*

Constables are to assist such Persons who have a Warrant from the Lieutenancy to search for Arms, *etc.* but it must be in the Day-time, unless in Towns; and if resisted, they may enter with Force; And High Constables, Petty Constables, *etc.* shall be assisted by others.

Arrests.

If a private Person arrest another, as in Case of dangerous Affrays, Suspicion, or knowing one to have committed Felony, or one that has violently wounded another, Night-Walkers that are dangerously suspicious, *etc.* which he may justify the doing; he ought to carry and deliver the Offender to a Constable, Headborough or Tithingman, and they are bound to secure the Party arrested. *10 Ed.4. c.6.; Dalt.468.*

Where Persons are arrested for Felony, if they are not delivered to a Constable, to be carried before a Justice, *etc.* it will be deemed an Escape. *Dalt.382.*

For Debt, *etc.* under £10 a Person shall not be arrested, but served with a Copy of the Process. *Stat. 12 Geo.1.*

Artificers.

Any Artificer contracting or preparing to go out of the Kingdom, on Complaint a Justice of Peace may send his Warrant to the Constable, *etc.* to bring the Party before him, and he may bind him over to the next Quarter-Sessions, where he must give Security not to depart the Realm. *Stat. 5 Geo.1. c.27.*

Not giving such Security, he shall be imprisoned; and Persons contracting with Artificers to go, shall be fined not exceeding £100 and suffer three Months Imprisonment.

Artificers going abroad, not returning in six Months after Warning given, are disabled to hold any Lands, *etc.*

Bakers.

Bakers not observing the Assise of Bread, are to be set on the Pillory, *etc. Stat. 51 H.3.*

By *8 Ann. c.18.* A Penalty of 40s. was inflicted on Bakers, selling Bread under Weight, deficient in Goodness, *etc.* But the *1 Geo.1. c.25.* enacts, that if any Baker shall make or expose to sale Bread wanting an Ounce of due Weight, he shall forfeit 5s. and wanting less than an Ounce 2s. 6d. to be levied by a Constable.

A Justice of Peace, Mayor, *etc.* may in the Day-time enter any Shop, Bakehouse, *etc.* to search for, and weigh and try Bread; and if the Bread be wanting in Goodness, or deficient in Weight, may seize the same, and give it to the Poor.

Bakers selling their Bread, consisting of Peck, Half peck, or Quartern Loaves, at a higher Price than set by the Lord Mayor of *London*, or by the Mayors, *etc.* of Towns, or two Justices of Peace, where there are no Mayors, shall forfeit 10s. to the Informer, to be levied by Distress by Constables, *etc. Stat. 3 Geo.2. c.29.*

Bastardy.

The Constable of a Parish is to apprehend Mothers of Bastard Children, that are likely to become chargeable to the Parish. *Dalt.*

A Constable may put a Person in the Stocks leaving a Child in any Parish, and not carrying it away being required, until such Time as he shall take up the Infant. *Poph. Rep. 12.*

Bawdy Houses.

A Constable having Information that Persons resort to a Common Bawdy House, and there keep Company with lewd Women, may, with others call'd to his Assistance, enter such House, and arrest the Offenders for a Breach of the Peace. *Mich. 13 H.7.* But he must find them in Company with lewd Women; and he is to carry them before a Justice of Peace, which he may do without Warrant, and the Justice may bind them to the Good Behaviour. *Dalt.214, 469.*

Bridges.

Where a Common Bridge is in Decay, and it cannot be known who are to repair it; the Constable and two of the most able Inhabitants in the Parish, are to make an Assessment, and four Justices of Peace to allow it. *22 H.8.*

Bridges ought to be repair'd by the Inhabitants of the whole Country, unless some particular Persons are bound thereto, by Reason of Tenure of Lands, *etc.*

All Bridges shall have Wall, or Posts and Rails on each Side four Feet high, and be kept sufficiently repaired. And the Taxation for Repairs of Bridges, shall not be made by the Justices, without Consent of the Constables or Inhabitants, nor by them without the Justices. *Stat. 14 Car.2. c.6.; 2 Co. Inst.704.*

Justices in Sessions, on Presentment that a Bridge is out of Repair, may assess every Town, Parish, *etc.* in Proportion towards the Reparation thereof; the Money assessed is to be levied by the Constables or Headboroughs, *etc.* by Distress and Sale, if not paid in ten Days; and then must be paid to the High Constables of Hundreds, who are to remit the same to Treasurers, *etc. Stat. 1 Ann. c.18.*

And if any of the Officers neglect to assess, collect or pay the Money, they shall forfeit 40s. Collectors, *etc.* of the Tax are to be allowed 3d. *per* Pound. *Ibid.*

On an Indictment for not Repairing of Bridges, a Fine may be set by the Justices in Sessions, upon any Inhabitant of the County, being made Defendant to the Indictment, who shall have Contribution from the rest. *6 Mod.307.*

Butter.

Justices of Peace in Sessions may restrain Retailing Butter and Cheese, which are to be sold in open Shop, *etc. 3 & 4 Ed.6. c.21.*

And corrupt Butter is not to be mix'd with good, on Pain to forfeit double the Value: Also Buyers of Butter are to set their Marks on Casks, *etc.* And if the Sellers open the Casks, or put in other Butter, after the Casks are thus mark'd, they are liable to the Penalty of 20s. leviable by a Constable. *14 Car.2.; 4 & 5 W. & M.*

Buttons.

By Virtue of a Justice's Warrant, Constables shall levy the Penalties on Taylors for making any Cloaths with Button or Button-Holes of Cloth, Stuff, *etc.* And also on the Wearers of the Cloaths, being 40s. *per* Dozen. *Stat. 4 & 7 Geo.1.*

Carriages.

When a Justice of Peace issues out Orders to Constables, to provide Carriages on the Marching of Soldiers, the Constables are to do it, being allowed by the

Officers, for a Waggon and five Horses, or for four Oxen and two Horses, or six Oxen, 1s. a Mile, and for a Cart and two Horses, 9d. *per* Mile. *Stat. 3 Geo.1. c.3.*

Officers obliging Constables to provide Saddle-Horses, forcing Horses from Owners, *etc.* or making a Carriage travel more than one Day, forfeit 5s. *Stat. Ibid.*

Constables neglecting or refusing to execute Justices Orders, or any other Person hindering the Execution thereof, shall forfeit not exceeding 40s. nor under 10s. to the Poor. *Stat. 3 Geo.1. c.3.*

No Waggon shall be oblig'd to carry above twenty Hundred Weight.

The Horses of Waggons, having more than their Number allow'd by Statute, which may be seized as forfeited, are to be deliver'd to Constables, *etc.* and by them re-deliver'd to the Seisor, on Conviction before a Justice. *Stat. 5 Geo.1. c.12.*

Cattle.

Constables, Tithingmen, Church-wardens, Overseers of the Poor, or any other Persons, may take and seize all Cattle, Sheep, Swine, Beef, Pork, Bacon, *etc.* brought from *Ireland*: And cause the said Cattle to be kill'd in six Days after Conviction of the Offence, and the Hides and Tallow shall be to the Seisor, and the Remainder to be distributed by the Church-wardens and Overseers amongst the Poor of the Parish where imported, or found. *Stat. 18 Car.2. c.2.; 20 Car.2. c.7.; 32 Car.2. c.2.*

Constables, or others seising Cattle, *etc.* imported out of *Ireland*, and not giving Notice in six Days after Conviction, to Church-wardens and Overseers, of such Seisure; and they not distributing all but the Hides and Tallow to the Poor, forfeit 40s. for every one of the great Cattle, and 13s. for every Sheep or Swine; one Moiety to the Poor, the other to the Informer; or to be committed to Gaol for three Months. *Stat. 32 Car.2. c.2.*

Cattle found alive in any other Parish after they have been seised, are liable to a second Seisure: And if there be any *English, Scotch,* or other Cattle intermix'd with *Irish,* they shall be forfeited.

Cloth and Clothiers.

Constables, on Request, are to be aiding and assisting to the Wardens and Assistants of the Weavers of *Norwich* Stuffs in the City of *Norwich* and County of *Norfolk,* in regulating that Part of the Cloathing Trade. *Stat. 14 Car.2. c.5.*

They are likewise, upon Request, to be assisting to the President, Wardens, *etc.* for regulating the Making of *Kidderminster* Stuffs, in the Borough of *Kidderminster. Stat. 22 & 23 Car.2. c.8.*

High Constables may hear and determine Complaints of Clothiers and their Work People; and commit the last till they make Satisfaction for Damages. *4 Ed.4.*

If any Person make Use of Flocks, Hair, or other deceitful Stuff in making Broad Cloth, on Certificate by two Justices, he shall forfeit £5 to be levied by Church-wardens and Overseers of the Poor, *etc.*

And Justices are to appoint Searchers of Cloth yearly, who shall fix their Seals to it, *etc. Stat. 39 Eliz.*

Spinsters, *etc.* imbezilling or detaining any Wool from Clothiers, shall make Satisfaction; or be whip'd and put in the Stocks by Constables, *etc. Stat. 7 Jac.1.*

c.7. It is made a Forfeiture of double Value, by *1 Ann.*

Broad Cloths are to contain the Quantity mention'd in the Seals, or the Seller shall forfeit a sixth Part. Millmen refusing to fix Seals, and others defacing or counterfeiting, *etc.* forfeit £20. Cloths are not to stretched above one Yard in Twenty in Length: They are to be measured by two indifferent Persons chosen by the Buyer and Seller, or on their Disagreement, by a Person appointed by chief Magistrates of Towns, *etc. Stat. 10 Ann. c.16.; 1 Geo.1. c.15.*

The Stat. *12 Geo.1. c.32.* was made against Combinations of Weavers, in the Cloathing Trade, for advancing their Wages, *etc.* and for punishing the same: And if any Weaver return his Work unfinish'd, *etc.* he shall be sent to the House of Correction for three Months.

Clothiers must pay their Work People their full Wages in Money, and not in Goods, on Pain of £10.

Clothiers are to give out all Wool, Yarn, *etc.* by Weight; and not use any Ends of Yarn, or other Refuse, by working them up again, under the Penalty of £5 leviable by Constables, by Warrant of two Justices of Peace. And Constables by such Warrant may enter and search Houses for Ends of Yarn, *etc. 13 Geo.*

Coals.

The Sack of Coal is to contain four Bushels of clean Coals: And Sea-Coals brought into the River *Thames*, and sold, shall be after the Rate of 36 Bushels to the Chaldron, *etc.* The Lord Mayor and Aldermen in *London*, and the Justices of the Peace of Counties, are empowered to set the Price of all Coals to be sold by Retail, and may appoint Officers to see them sold at the Rates appointed. *7 Ed.6. c.7.; 16 & 17 Car.2. c.2.*

And by the late Act for regulating the Coal Trade, Sellers of Coals are to keep a lawful Bushel edg'd with Iron, and Seal'd or Stamp'd; and using other Measures, or altering them, incurs a Forfeiture of £50. There must be three Bushels to each Sack; and the Sacks are to be mark'd, and be four Feet and two Inches in Length, and twenty-six Inches in Breadth, on Pain of 20s. *etc. Stat. 3 Geo.2. c.26.*

The Penalties under £5 inflicted by this Statute, are recoverable on Complaint before the Lord Mayor of *London*, or any Justices of Peace, to be levied by Distress by Constables, *etc.* And for want thereof the Offenders shall be committed to the House of Correction, not exceeding thirty Days. *Stat. Ibid.*

Conventicles.

Constables, Headboroughs, Tithingmen, Church-wardens, *etc.* are required to levy the Fines imposed on those, who shall be present at unlawful Conventicles, by Virtue of a Warrant under the Hand of one or more Justices. *22 Car.2. c.1.*

Constables, *etc.* knowing, or being credibly informed, of any Conventicle within their Precincts, and not giving Information thereof to some Justice of Peace, or chief Magistrate, and endeavouring to convict the Persons, forfeit £5. *22 Car.2. c.1.*

On Information given of Conventicles, Constables, *etc.* with Aid and Assistance, may, by Virtue of a Warrant from one or more Justice or Justices, or chief Magistrate, (upon Refusal to enter) break open Doors, and enter into any House or Place, where they are informed such Conventicles are held, and take into Custody Persons unlawfully assembled. *Ibid. Stat.*

The Compleat Parish Officer - Constables.

The Houses of Peers not to be search'd, unless in the Presence of the Lord Lieutenant, or two Justices of the Peace. And Protestant *Dissenters* are excepted out of this Act. *Stat. 1 W. & M. c.24.* But if any Assembly of Dissenters shall be held in any Place, with the Doors lock'd or bolted during the Time of Service; they are liable to Prosecution, as others, notwithstanding taking the Oaths, *etc.* directed by the Act *1 W. & M.*

Any Person sued for acting according to the *Stat. 22 Car.2.* may plead the General Issue, and give the special Matter in Evidence, and recover treble Costs. *Stat. 22 Car.2. c.1.*

Customs.

Customs are certain Duties and Impositions upon Goods and Merchandize imported and exported, payable to the Crown.

And Constables, *etc.* are to be assisting to all Persons appointed by the King for the Collecting and Managing of the Customs. *Stat. 14 Car.2. c.2.*

They are, upon Request, to assist Persons having a Warrant from the Lord Treasurer, Barons of the Exchequer, or Chief Magistrates of Ports, to make a Search for Goods which have not paid the Customs; and may enter into any House in the Day-time, and if refused, break open Doors. But this last must be within a Month after the Offence committed. *Stat. 12 Car.2. c.19.*

Ships are not to take in, or unlade any Goods, till entered with the Collector of the Customs; and if Goods are put into any Vessel, to be carried beyond Sea, *etc.* and the Duties not paid or agreed, the same shall be forfeited, one Moiety to the King, and the other to the Seisor, *etc. Stat. 12 Car.2.* and *13 & 14 Car.2.*

And foreign Goods taken in at Sea by any coasting Vessel, *etc.* are liable to Forfeiture and treble Value: But Custom-house Officers making collusive Seizures, shall forfeit £500. *Stat. 5 Geo.1. c.11.*

Officers of the Customs hindered in the Execution of their Offices by Persons armed, to the Number of Eight, the Offenders to be transported for seven Years. *Stat. 6 Geo.1. c.20.* against Running of Goods.

Deer-Stealing.

The Penalties on Deer-Stealers are to be levied by Constables, by Virtue of a Warrant from a Justice of Peace; and Constables may detain Offenders two Days, if they do not pay the Forfeitures down upon Conviction, until a Return may be made of the Warrant of Distress. *Stat. 13 Car.2. c.10.*

The Forfeitures are £20 for Coursing or Hunting Deer in any Park or Place inclos'd, and £30 for every Deer taken, wounded, and killed; one third Part to the Poor, another to the Informer, and the other Third to the Owner of the Deer. *Stat. 13 Car.2. cap.10.; 3 & 4 W. & M.*

Constables may enter any suspected Place, and carry away Venison, Skins of Deer, Toils, *etc.* by Warrant from one Justice, and likewise carry the Offender before the Justice, to give an Account how he came by the same.

By *Stat. 5 Geo.1. c.15.* Park-Keepers killing Deer without Consent of Owners, shall forfeit £50. And Persons pulling down Walls, *etc.* of Parks, are liable to the Penalties for killing Deer.

Deer-Stealers convicted before a Judge of Gaol Delivery, may be sent to the

Plantations for seven Years, by this Statute.

And if any Persons arm'd with Swords, Fire-Arms, or other Weapons, and having their Faces *black'd*, *etc.* shall appear in any Forest or Park, and unlawfully hunt or kill any Deer, rob any Warren, *etc.* it is Felony without Benefit of Clergy. *Stat. 9 Geo.1. c.22.* **See *Riots*.**

Deserters.

Any Constable, *etc.* has Power to take up a Person suspected of Desertion, and to bring him before a Justice; and if, upon Examination, it shall appear that he is a listed *Soldier*, the Justice shall commit him to the County-Gaol, and give an Account thereof to the Secretary at War. *Stat. 1 Geo.1. c.3.*

Distillers.

Constables shall be assisting to the Officers of Excise, in entering the Houses of Distillers to make search after and seise unlawful Stills; and they are to levy the Penalties for setting up any private Still, Tun, Pipe, *etc.* by Virtue of a Justice's Warrant. *Stat. 3 & 4 W. & M.; 10 & 11 W.3. c.4.*

Distillers are to pay certain Duties, and make an Entry of all Ware-houses, Still-houses, *etc.* And Persons hawking or selling Brandy about Streets in Wheel-barrows, or on any Bulk, Shed, *etc.* shall forfeit £10 leviable by Constables, by Warrant of Justices, *etc. Stat. 6 Geo.2. c.17.*

Distress.

The Constable, in taking Distresses, is to assist the Landlord or Person distraining; as where any Goods or Chattels shall be taken in Distress for any Rent reserved, and due upon any Demise, Lease, or Contract; and the Tenant and Owner of the Goods shall not within five Days, after such Distress taken, and Notice thereof given, and of the Cause, left at the Dwelling-house or most notorious Place on the Premises charg'd with the Rent distrain'd for, replevy the same according to Law: Then the Landlord, or Person distraining , may with the Sheriff or Under-Sheriff of the County, or with the Constable of the Hundred, Parish, or Place where the Distress shall be taken, (who are requir'd to be aiding and assisting therein) cause the Goods and Chattels to be apprais'd by two sworn Appraisers, and afterwards sell the same for the best Price, towards Satisfaction of the Rent and Charges of the Distress, Appraisement and Sale, leaving the Overplus in the Sheriff's or Constable's Hands for the Use of the Owner. *Stat. 2 W. & M.*

N.B. The Under-Sheriff, Constables, *etc.* have Power to administer an Oath to the Appraisers.

Appraiser's Oath.

You shall swear, that you will faithfully appraise and value the Goods now taken in Distress, and mentioned in the Inventory to you shewn, as between Buyer and Seller, according to the best of your Skill and Understanding: You shall not through Partiality, Interest, or otherwise, over or under Estimate the said Goods, but impartially do your Duties herein. So help you God.

If Tenants fraudulently convey away Goods from off the Premises, the Landlord, *etc.* may in five Days, seise such Goods wheresoever found, as a Distress for the Rent in Arrear; except *bona fide* sold for a valuable Consideration, by Stat. *8 Ann. c.17.*

Dogs. See Title *Game.*

Drunkenness.

Constables are to levy the Sum of 5s. on Persons convicted of Drunkenness, for the Use of the Poor: And if the Party is not able to pay it, he must be set in the Stocks six Hours, etc. *Stat. 4 Jac.1. c.5.; 21 Jac.1. c.7.*

Neglecting to levy the said Penalty upon Warrant from one Justice, to forfeit 10s. *4 Jac.1. c.5.*

Constables, Tithingmen, Church-wardens, *etc.* are to present and suppress Drunkenness, by the Stat. *21 Jac.1.*

Dyers.

The Penalties inflicted on Dyers, for dying Cloth deceitfully, being in Proportion to the Length and Goodness of the Cloths, are to be levied by Warrant of two or more Justices, by Constables, *etc.* if not paid in twenty Days. *Stat. 13 Geo.1. c.24.*

Forfeitures within ten Miles of *London*, shall go one Moiety to the Dyers Company, and the other to the Informer; and beyond that the whole to the Informer. *Ibid.*

Excise.

As to this Head relating to Liquors, Constables, upon Warrants to them directed, are to summon all Alehouse-Keepers, *etc.* to appear before the Commissioners of Excise.

Officers of Excise are to take with them a Constable, when they enter into a Brew-house, *etc.* by Night to gauge Fats or Vessels. *Stat. 12 Car.2. c.23.*

Brewers refusing a Gauger to enter in the Night with a Constable, forfeit £20 and Makers or Retailers of Cyder, Vinegar, *etc.* £15.

Excisemen suspecting a secret Conveyance of Worts, may, upon Request, and in Presence of a Constable, break open a Door in the Day-time to make a Discovery. *Stat. 7 & 8 W. & M. c.30.*

Persons opposing them forfeit £20. Brewers keeping private Houses, or altering any Tuns, Vessels, *etc.* without giving Notice, forfeit £50 one Third to the King, another to the Informer, and the other Third to the Poor. *15 Car.2.; 1 W. & M. c.24.; 8 & 9 W.3.*

Constables, by Warrant from Justices, are to levy the Penalty on Offenders against any Law of Excise, by Distress, *etc.* And if there be no Distress, to carry them to Gaol, there to remain until Satisfaction be made. *Stat. 12 Car.2. c.23.; 1 W. & M.*

Escapes.

If a Constable permits a Felon to escape before he is arrested, it is a Misdemeanor, for which he may be indicted, and fined; and if the Felon be actually taken and in Custody, and then he voluntarily suffers him to escape, or to kill or destroy himself, it is Felony in the Constable: But if the Escape is by Negligence, or involuntary, or the Felon destroys himself unawares to the Constable, it is only fineable. *Dalt.379.; Cro. Eliz. 752.*

A Constable may pursue an Offender making an Escape into another County, and bring him back to the Justice of Peace. *Cromp.148, 173, etc.* He may put a

Felon in the Stocks, and lock him in; or put Irons upon him, or pinion him, to prevent an Escape, when he is about to carry him before a Justice of Peace, or to Gaol. *Dalt.342.*

He may discharge any Person arrested on Suspicion of Felony only, where no Felony is committed; but if a Felony be actually committed, he cannot justify the Discharging him, though he know that the Party is innocent; but it must be done by due Course of Law, otherwise it will be an Escape. *Cromp.40.; Cro. Eliz. 202.*

See *Gaol* and *Gaolers.*

Felons.

A Constable is bound *ex officio* to endeavour to apprehend Felons; and any Offence that is in Degree next to Treason, is Felony; as Murder, Robbery, Theft, Sodomy, Rape, *etc.* He may raise Men to assist him, apprehend Persons on Suspicion, and carry them before a Justice to be examin'd; and upon Complaint, or Common Fame, he may search suspicious Houses, both for the Felon and Goods stolen. And Officers may break open a House to take a Felon, or any one suspected thereof. *Dalt.332.*

If Felons or Murderers be in a Town or Village, and the Constable, Headborough, *etc.* have Notice of it, they are to command Assistance, and apprehend them; and afterwards it is the Constable's Business to see them conveyed to Gaol. *1 R.3.*

If a Felon fly, the Constable is to seise and make an Inventory of his Goods, and send Hue and Cry after him; that is, he may raise the Town, and give Notice to the next Constable, *etc.* And if upon such Flight, he is apprehended in another County, he must be carry'd before a Justice of that County where taken, and committed to Gaol there, and not in the County where the Fact was done. *Stat. 13 Ed.3. c.3.; 27 Eliz. 13.*

Constable neglecting, is fineable by the Justices.

Persons convicted of Felony, Larceny, *etc.* within the Benefit of Clergy, to be sent to the Plantations for seven Years, instead of being whipt, or burnt in the Hand; and for Crimes, excluded Clergy may be transported for 14 Years. Returning without Licence, *etc.* they are to suffer Death. *Stat. 4 Geo.1. c.11, etc.*

Persons taking Money for helping others to stolen Goods, and not prosecuting the Felon, to be guilty of Felony. *Stat. Ibid.*

Any Person may arrest one that has committed Felony.

Fish.

Constables, *etc.* are to levy the Penalty of 10s. for the Poor, and treble Damages, for fishing in a River without the Owner's Consent. *Stat. 22 & 23 Car.2.*

To levy the Penalty of 10s. upon Persons fishing in Nets of less Meshes than three Inches and a Half from Knot to Knot, on the Sea-Coast, or in any Haven or Creek, or within five Miles thereof; or using Engines to destroy the Breed of Fish, by Warrant from a Justice of Peace. *3 Jac.1. c.12.*

They are to search likewise, by Virtue of a Justice's Warrant, in *Shropshire*, *Worcestershire*, and *Gloucestershire*, for unlawful Nets used to take Fish in the *Severn*, and to seise such Nets, and carry them to the Quarter-Sessions, to be destroyed. *Stat. 30 Car.2. cap.9.*

Fishmongers of *London* ingrossing *Billinsgate* Market, or buying any Quantity of Fish there, but what shall be for their own Sale and Use, forfeit £20 one Moiety to the Poor, the other to the Prosecutor. *Stat. 10 & 11 W.3.*

No Salmon shall be taken between the 1st of *August* and the 12th of *November*, in Rivers, in the Counties of *Southampton* and *Wilts*; nor Salmon or Trout under Size, *etc.* under a Penalty not less than 20s. nor above £5 leviable by Distress by Constables, *etc. 4 & 5 Ann. c.21.*

Salmon bought by Fishmongers are to be six Pounds Weight, under the Penalty of £5 and Fish sold to be of certain Lengths, as Bret and Turbet sixteen Inches, Brill and Pearl fourteen Inches, Codlin twelve Inches, Flounder seven Inches, Whiting six Inches, *etc.* under the Penalty of 20s. *Stat. 1 Geo.1. cap.18.*

Forcible Entry.

Forcible Entry is a violent Entring into, and Detaining the Possession of Houses, Lands, *etc.* And at Common Law, where a Man had Title to Lands, he might not only enter, but detain by Force: But the *Stat. 5 R.2. c.7.* prohibits the Force, though a Person have Title.

This Statute enacts, That Justices of Peace shall enquire into the Force; and if Constables refuse to assist the Justices in removing the Force, or carrying Offenders to Gaol, they may be committed and fined. *15 R.2.*

Justices of Peace may cause the Tenements to be seised; and have Power to award Restitution, where Lands are detain'd by Force. *Stat. 8 H.6. c.9.; 21 Jac.1. c.15.*

Foreign Goods Imported.

Constables, upon Warrants to them directed by a Justice of Peace, are to search for foreign Bonelace, Embroidery, Needlework, Fringe, Buttons, *etc.* in Shops, open Warehouses, and Dwelling-houses, and to seise them. *Stat. 13 & 14 Car.2. c.2.*

Persons importing, selling or offering to Sale such foreign Manufactures, forfeit £100 for importing, and £50 for selling, and the Goods; one Moiety to the King, the other to the Prosecutor.

Constables were likewise, during the late War with *France*, to be assisting in the Execution of the Act, prohibiting the Importation of *French* Wines, and other foreign Trade with that Kingdom.

Forestallers.

Forestallers of Markets, and Ingrossers and Regrators are punishable by Justices of Peace in their Quarter-Sessions, on the Presentment of Constables, *etc.*

And a Forestaller by Statute is declared to be one who buys Victuals, or Merchandize, *etc.* by the Way, before it is brought to a Fair or Market, to the Intent to sell the same at a higher Price: A Regrator is one that buys any Grain, Butter, Cheese, *etc.* in a Fair or Market, and sells the same in the same Market, or within four Miles: And an Ingrosser is one who buys Corn growing, *etc.* or Butter, or Cheese, with Intent to sell again. *Stat. 5 & 6 Ed.6. c.14.*

These Offenders shall forfeit for the first Offence the Value of the Goods, and suffer two Months Imprisonment; for the second Offence double the Penalty, *etc.* and for the third Offence shall lose all their Goods, and be set on the Pillory, *etc.*

Ibid.

But Maltsters buying Barley, Badgers of Corn, Butchers, and Poulterers, *etc.* are excepted out of the Act.

Game.

Constables shall carry Higlers, Chapmen, Inn-Keepers, Victuallers, *etc.* before a Justice, for having in their Custody Hare, Pheasant, Partridge, Heath Game, or other Game; or Persons as shall buy or sell any such; who shall forfeit £5 for every Hare, *etc.* one Half to the Poor, and the other to the Informer. *Stat. 5 Ann. c.14.*

Constables, by Warrant from a Justice, may enter and search the Houses of Persons suspected, not qualified to kill Game; and if they find any Game there, shall carry the Offender before the Justice; and if they meet with any Dogs, Nets, *etc.* may take away and destroy them. *22 & 23 Car.2. c.25.; 4 & 5 W. & M. c.23.*

Constables may carry any Person not qualified before a Justice, for keeping of Greyhounds, Setting-Dogs, *etc.* and on Conviction they shall forfeit £5. *Stat. 5 Ann.* and *3 Geo.1. cap.11.*

Persons qualified to keep Guns, *etc.* and kill Game, are such as have a free Warren, Lords of Manors, or who have £100 *per Annum* of Inheritance, either in their own Right, or in the Right of their Wives, or for Life; or Lease for 99 Years of £150 *per Annum*; a Son and Heir of an Esquire, or one of higher Dignity. *Stat. 22 & 23 Car.2. c.25.* And Persons thus qualified may take Guns, *etc.* from those that are not. By *Stat. 33 H.8. c.6.* Persons keeping Guns, not being qualified, forfeit £10.

The *22 & 23 Car.2.* empowers Lords of Manors to appoint Game-keepers. And by *9 Ann.* and *3 Geo.1.* Game-keepers are to be entered with the Clerk of the Peace; to be qualified, or be Servants to Lords of Manors, under the like Penalties as for unlawful killing of Game. See *Stat. 8 Geo.1. c.19.*

A Warrant from a Lord of a Manor to a Game-keeper.

To all People to whom these Presents shall come, I A.B. of, etc. Esq; Lord of the Manor of, etc. in the County of, etc. have nominated, authorized and appointed, and by these Presents do nominate, authorize, and appoint C.D. of, etc. to be my Game-keeper, of and within my Manor of, etc. aforesaid, with full Power and Authority, according to the Direction of the Statutes in that Case made and provided, to kill Game for my Use, and to take and seize all such Guns, Greyhounds, Setting-Dogs, and other Dogs, Ferrets, Trammels, Hays, or other Nets, Snares or Engines, for the Taking, Killing or destroying of Hares, Pheasants, Partridges, or other Game, as within the said Manor of, etc. and the Precincts thereof, shall be kept or used by any Person or Persons not legally qualified to do the same: And further, to do all and every Thing and Things which belong to the Office of a Game-keeper, according to the Direction of the said Acts of Parliament; for which this shall be his sufficient Warrant. Given, etc.

Enter'd the Day, *etc.*   *Per I. W. Cler' Pac'.*

Gaming.

Mayors, Constables, and other Head Officers, are to make Search once a Month where unlawful Games shall be kept; and may arrest and imprison the Masters of the Houses, and the Gamesters, 'till they give Security not to do the like for the

Future: The Master forfeits 40s. a Day. *Stat. 33 H.8. c.9.* There is a Penalty likewise of 6s. 8d. for using unlawful Games; and on Default of Payment, the Offender to be set in the Stocks three Hours. Constables neglecting their Duties, forfeit 40s. for every Default.

Tables, Tennis, Bowls, Cards, Dice, *etc.* are declared unlawful Games, by the said Statute; but this extends only to Artificers, Apprentices, Journeymen, Servants, *etc.*

Persons having no visible Estates, not making it appear that the principal Part of their Maintenance is got by other Means than Gaming, are to be bound to the good Behaviour, being carried before a Justice of Peace by a Constable, *etc.*

If a Person lose by Gaming £10 at one Time, he may recover the same back from the Winner. *Stat. 9 Ann. c.14.*

Gaol and Gaolers.

When a Constable carries a Felon, or one suspected of Felony to Gaol, the Gaoler is obliged to receive him; but if he refuses to do it, then the Constable may either secure the Prisoner in his own House, or carry him back to the Town where apprehended; and the Town shall be chargeable for the Keeping of him 'till the next Gaol-delivery, where the Gaoler shall be punished. *10 Hen.4.; Dalt.310.*

Constables by Warrant from a Justice of Peace, may sell an Offender's Goods to defray the Charges of carrying him to Gaol, being first appraised by some of the Inhabitants of the Place: But if the Offender hath no Goods, then the Town where he was apprehended must be at the Expence; and the Constable and Church-wardens, and two or more of the Inhabitants may impose a Tax, take a Distress for it, after allowed by a Justice, and sell the Distress when appraised by four Inhabitants. *Stat. 3 Jac.1. c.10.*

If a Prisoner escape from Gaol by the Negligence of his Keeper, and against his Consent, it is Felony in the Prisoner for the Breach of Prison; and the Gaoler is fineable. *Dalt.379.; Staunds. 32, 34.* If voluntary in the Gaoler, it is Felony in him.

Constables are to levy Money for Reparation of Gaols, by Warrant from Justices. *Stat. 11 & 12 W.3. c.19.*

Gunpowder.

In *London* and *Westminster, etc.* Constables, by Virtue of a Warrant from two Justices of Peace, may search for Gunpowder in any Storehouse, *etc.* in the Day-time, where Persons keep a greater Quantity than is allowed by Law; and Justices of Peace on Demand by any Parish-Officer, or two Housholders, assigning Cause, shall issue Warrants for Search, and Amoval, *etc.*

Persons obstructing the Search, or Amoval, forfeit £5.

The Quantity of Gunpowder to be kept, is not to exceed 200 *lb.* Weight, on Pain of forfeiting the same: And Gunpowder must be carried in covered Carriages, *etc. Stat. 5 & 11 Geo.1. c.23.*

No Gunpowder shall be put on board Ships, above *Blackwall* in the River of *Thames*; nor Guns kept loaded, or fired before Rising or after Setting of the Sun, under the Penalty of £5 to be levied by Constables, by Justices Warrant, *etc. Stat. 5 Geo.2. c.20.*

Ships of War are excepted out of the Act.

Guns. *Vide* Title *Game.*

Hawkers.

Constables refusing to assist in putting the Laws in Execution against Hawkers, *etc.* forfeit 40s. one Moiety to the Poor.

Hawkers, Pedlars, *etc.* travelling without a Licence, shall forfeit £12 and refusing to shew their Licences forfeit £5. *Stat. 8 & 9 W.3.* Any Person may Seize a Hawker 'till he produce a Licence.

On granting Licences, Hawkers, *etc.* on Foot, pay £4. And if with Horse, Ass, or Mule, £8 Duty to the King. But Makers of Goods, selling those of their own making; Sellers of Almanacks, Acts of Parliament, *etc.* and of Fruit, Victuals, *etc.* are excepted out of the Acts against Hawkers. *Stat. 8 & 9 W.3. c.25.; 3 & 4 Ann. c.4.*

Hay-market.

For Carts of Hay which stand to be sold in the Hay-market, so much *per* Load is to be paid towards the Paving and Amending the Street; and they shall not stand laden after Three a-Clock in the Afternoon, *etc.* under the Penalty of 5s. And Persons selling Trusses of Hay wanting due Weight, shall forfeit for every Truss 2s. 6d. to be levied by Constables, by Warrant of a Justice. *Stat. 2 W. & M. cap.8.*

Hedge-breakers, etc.

Hedge-breakers, Robbers of Orchards, Persons cutting Corn growing, *etc.* committed to a Constable by a Justice of Peace, for not making the Party Satisfaction for Damages, are to be whipt by the Constable for the first Offence; and if the Constable neglect his Duty, the Justice may commit him without Bail 'till the Offender is whipped. Procurers and Receivers of stolen Wood, *etc.* knowing the same, are liable to the same Punishment. *Stat. 43 Eliz. c.7.*

Constables have Power to apprehend Persons suspected of Hedge-breaking, having in their Possession any Underwood, Poles, young Trees, Gates, Stiles, Posts, Rails, *etc.* And by Warrant from a Justice of Peace, to enter the Houses of suspected Persons; and if they find any, then to take the Offenders, and those in whose Houses, *etc.* the Wood is found, and carry them before a Justice. *Stat. 15 Car.2. c.2.*

Not giving a good Account how they came by the same, to make such Recompence to the Party grieved as the Justice shall appoint, and pay a Sum not exceeding 10s. for the Use of the Poor; and in Default, to be sent to the House of Correction for any Time not exceeding a Month, or be whipped by the Constable. *Stat. Ibid.* Buyers of stolen Wood, to pay treble the Value to the Party from whom taken.

By a late Statute, Persons maliciously cutting or spoiling Timber-Trees, Fruit Trees, or other Trees, are to be sent to the House of Correction for three Months, there to be kept at hard Labour, and publicly whipped once in every Month. *1 Geo.1. c.48.* Burning Timber or Underwood, is made Felony by this Statute.

Where Trees, Woods, *etc.* are destroyed, or Hedges, Gates, *etc.* broke open; the Owners shall have Satisfaction from the Inhabitants of the Place, *etc.* if the Offender be not convicted in six Months. *Stat. 6 Geo.1. c.16.*

Highways.

By ancient Statutes, Constables were yearly on *Tuesday* or *Wednesday* in *Easter* Week, to call together the Inhabitants of Parishes, and chuse two Surveyors of the Highways for the next Year, or they were liable to be fin'd in Quarter-Sessions. *2 & 3 Ph. & M. c.8.*

But now by the Statute *3 & 4 W. & M.* Constables, Church-wardens, *etc.* and Inhabitants are injoined to meet the Day after *Christmas* Day, and the greater Part of them so met, to agree on Persons qualified to serve the Office of Surveyor; a List of which the Constable must return to the Justices of Peace at a special Sessions, on the 3d of *January* following, in order to their Appointment of Surveyors; under the Penalty of 20s. The like Penalty for the Constables not serving such Surveyors with the Justices Warrant within six Days after Appointment.

Constables and Church-wardens have Power to call a Bailiff, or a High Constable to account for Fines received for Defaults in Reparation of Ways, on Presentments, *etc.* And if he should refuse to pass his Account, they may summon him before two Justices, who may commit him 'till he has satisfied all the Arrears, except 8d. in the Pound for his own Fee for collecting, and 1s. in the Pound for the Clerk of the Peace. *2 & 3 Ph. & M.*

By Statute *22 Car.2. cap. 12.* All Constables, as well as Surveyors, are to put the Act in Execution relating to the Repairing and Inlarging of Highways, on Pain of forfeiting a Sum not exceeding 40s. at the Discretion of a Justice of Peace. And are to levy the Penalties relating to Scavengers, and Defaults in cleaning the Streets of *London, etc.*

See *Surveyors of Highways, etc.* post.

Horses.

Constables are to assist at *Michaelmas*, or within fifteen Days after, in the Driving of Commons, Forests, *etc.* of Horses and Cattle on Pain of 40s. *Stat. 32 H.8. c.13.*

They are likewise to assist in the Seizing of ston'd Horses, put into Commons where Mares are usually kept, not being of the Age of two Years, and fifteen Hands high (except in Fen Grounds, where thirteen Hands high is allowed) and in the Measuring of them at the next Pound, to which they are to be brought for that Purpose, on Pain of forfeiting 40s.

Fens in the Counties of *Cambridge, Huntingdon, Nottingham, Lincoln, Norfolk,* and *Suffolk*, are excepted.

Hue and Cry.

Hue and Cry, as I have already defined in the Head *Felons*, is a Raising of a Town or Country for the Pursuing and apprehending of an Offender, where a Felony is committed, and he flies for the same; and is most commonly made for Robbery on the Highway.

The Manner of making Hue and Cry is thus: The Constable, on the Felon's being described, and Information given which Way he is gone, is to call upon the Parishioners to assist him in the Pursuit in his Precinct; and if the Offender be not there, he is to give Notice to the next Constable, (who is to do the like as the first) and he to the next, and so to be made from Town to Town, and County to County, by Horsemen and Footmen to the Sea-side; unless the Offender in the Pursuit is sooner apprehended: And, in the mean Time, the first Constable is to make an Inventory of his Goods in the Presence of his Neighbours. *Stat. 13 Ed.1. cap.3.; 27 Eliz. cap.13.*

Constables and Officers of every Town to which Hue and Cry shall come, are to make diligent Search in all suspected Houses and Places within their Limits; and not only Officers, but all others who shall pursue the Hue and Cry, may arrest all such Persons as in their Search and Pursuit they shall find suspicious, and carry them before some Justice of Peace of the County where taken, to be examined where they were at the Time of the Felony committed. *13 Ed.1. cap.1.*

Constables neglecting their Duty, may be indicted and fined.

Inhabitants of any Hundred where Hue and Cry is made, neglecting to pursue it, shall answer one Moiety of the Damages recoverable against the Hundred, where the Robbery is committed. *Stat. 27 Eliz. c.13.*

See more, Title *Felons.*

Inns and Inn-keepers

Inns are allowed for the Relief and Lodging of Travellers: But they are to be licensed and regulated by Justices of Peace, *etc.* And if a Person sets up an Inn, in a Place where there is no Need of one; or keep it in a Situation wholly unfit for it; or harbours Thieves, *etc.* he may be indicted and fined. *Dalt.33, 34.*

Inn-keepers are to sell all Kinds of Victuals for Man and Beast, at reasonable Prices, having Respect to the Price sold in the Markets adjoining, without taking any Thing for Horse Litter; or they shall be fined and imprisoned; and for a third Offence may be put in the Pillory; by *Stat. 21 Jac.1. c.21.*

And if a common Inn-keeper or Alehouse-keeper shall refuse to lodge a Traveller, or to provide him Victuals, *etc.* who offers to pay ready Money for the same; the Constable, on Complaint, is to cause such Inn-keeper, *etc.* to be indicted at the next Sessions, where the Justices may punish him by Fine and Imprisonment. *10 Hen.7. c.8.*

If the Traveller does not approve this Method of Proceeding, he may prosecute the Inn-keeper by Action at Law, in any of the Courts at *Westminster*, and recover Damages. *Dalt. f.30.*

And it is said, the Constable of the Town may compel an Inn-keeper, to receive and entertain such a Traveller as his Guest. *1 Hawk.225.*

Juries.

At *Michaelmas* Sessions yearly, Constables, *etc.* are to give in to the Justices of Peace a List of the Names and Places of Habitation (within their respective Limits) of all Persons qualified to serve on Juries, between the Age of 21 and 70; and Sheriffs shall impanel no others, *etc. Stat. 7 & 8 W.3. c.32.*

The Qualifications are £80 *per Ann.* Freehold, for a Grand Juryman; and £10 *per Ann.* Freehold or Copyhold, for a Petty Juryman; except it be in Corporations, where a Freeman worth £40 in Goods, may serve on the Petty Jury, by *Stat. 23 H.8.*

But Aliens, Apothecaries, Butchers, Clergymen, Infants, Persons attainted of any Crime, *etc.* may not serve on Juries.

Constables neglecting to return Lists of Names of Persons fit to serve on Juries, shall forfeit £5. And by the Statute *3 & 4 A. c.18*. High Constables are to issue their Precepts to the Petty Constables, to prepare such Lists, by Virtue of a Warrant from Justices in the Sessions, under the Penalty of £10.

Lists of Jurors qualified are to be made from the Rates of each Parish, and yearly fix'd on the Doors of Churches, *etc*. twenty Days before the Feast of St. *Michael*, that publick Notice may be given thereof; and returning Officers, as Constables, *etc*. wilfully omitting Persons qualified, or inserting wrong Persons, shall forfeit 20s. By *Stat. 3 Geo.2. cap.25*.

Constables must subscribe their Lists, and attest the Truth of them on Oath before one or more Justices of Peace; and then deliver them to the High Constables of the Hundreds, who are to deliver them attested to the Justices in Sessions; And Duplicates of the Lists when adjusted by the Justices, are to be delivered by the Clerks of the Peace to the Sheriffs of Counties.

Sheriffs are to enter the Names of the Persons in a Book alphabetically, with their Additions, and Places of Abode, *etc*. And returning any other Persons to serve upon Juries, shall be fined by the Judges of Assise not exceeding £10 nor less than 40s. The like Penalty for taking Money to excuse Persons from serving: And Jurors not appearing, unless reasonable Cause of Absence be proved, to be fined not above £5 or under 40s. *Stat. Ibid.*

By this Act Persons having Estates held by Lease for 500 Years, or 99 Years, or any other Term determinable on Lives, *etc*. of the yearly Value of £20 are qualified to serve on Juries; And none shall be returned as Jurymen in *London*, but Householders having Lands or Personal Estate to the Value of £100.

The Juries for Trial of Causes are to be chosen by Ballot, by drawing Papers with the Names of the Jurors summoned, rolled up in a Box, *etc*. And in Trials on Indictments, *etc*. and all Actions, the Courts at *Westminster* may order a special Jury, by this new Statute.

Labourers.

A Constable, *ex officio*, may in Hay or Corn Harvest Time, set Artificers and ordinary Tradesmen on Work by the Day, (being requir'd by Persons who want Labourers) and put those in the Stocks for two Days and a Night who refuse; and the Constable neglecting his Duty herein, forfeits 40s. *Stat. 5 Eliz. cap.4*.

From the Middle of *March* to the Middle of *September*, Labourers are to work from Five in the Morning until Seven a Clock at Night, being allow'd two Hours for Breakfast and Dinner, *etc*. and Half an Hour for sleeping, the three hot Months; and all the rest of the Year from Twilight to Twilight, except an Hour and an Half for Breakfast and Dinner; on Pain of forfeiting 1d. an hour. *5 Eliz.*

Labourers conspiring together concerning their Work or Wages, shall forfeit for the first Offence £10 for the second £20, and for the third Offence £40 or be set on the Pillory, *etc. 2 & 3 Ed.6*.

And taking Work by the Great, and leaving it unfinish'd, unless for Non-payment of Wages, *etc*. they shall suffer one Month's Imprisonment, and forfeit £5. *Stat. 5 Eliz. c.4*.

And if any Labourers wander abroad out of their Parishes, and refuse to work for reasonable Wages, *etc*. they are declared Vagrants by the *Stat. 12 Ann*.

Lamps. See *Scavengers.*
Land-Tax.

In collecting the Land-Tax, Constables are to be assisting; and where it is refused Payment they are to take a Distress, *etc.* and in the Day-time, with the Collectors, Constables may justify Breaking open Houses, by Virtue of a Warrant from the Commissioners. *Stat. 1 W. & M.*

Where Lands or Houses are unoccupied, and no Distress to be found, whereby the Parish, *etc.* is charged; the Collectors, Constable, or Tithingmen of the Parish, or Place, may at any Time after take a Distress upon the Lands, or in the Houses, to reimburse the Parish: And if such Distress be not redeemed within four Days, they may sell the same, and distribute the Money amongst the Parties who contributed to the Tax proportionably, rendring the Overplus to the Owner.

Wood may be cut at seasonable Times in the Year; and Tithes, Tolls, or annual Profits not distrainable, may be seised and sold for Satisfaction of the Tax; where Assessments are made upon such Wood-lands, or Tithes, *etc.*

Commissioners are appointed for Counties, *etc.* to levy this Tax, who nominate Assessors, and they return Collectors in every Parish; the Collectors detaining the Money, shall be imprison'd, and their Estates sold; and Receivers General, not returning the same, are liable to £500 Penalty. *Stat. 1 Geo.1.*

The Receiver General is allowed a Fee of 2d. in the Pound, the Collectors 3d. *per* Pound, and Three Half-pence to the Commissioners Clerks.

Leather. Vide *Shoemakers.*
Malt.

Constables, *etc.* have Power to inspect the making of Malt. They are to search for bad Malt; and if they find any deceitfully made, or mingled bad with good, they may, with the Advice of a Justice, cause the same to be sold at reasonable Rates, discretionary in the Justice. *Stat. 2 & 3 Edw.6. cap.10.*

Malt is adjudged ill made, when it is not steeping, making and drying three Weeks; if Half a Peck of Dust is not skreened or fanned out of every Quarter; if it be made of mowburnt, or spired Barley.

There is a Forfeiture inflicted by the Statute *supra*, of 2s. for every Quarter of Malt consisting of bad and good mingled together, and put to Sale, to be divided between the King and Prosecutor; and 20d. *per* Quarter, where Half a Peck of Dust is not taken by treading or rubbing, *etc.* Prosecution to be in a Year.

A Duty of 6d. *per* Bushel is granted on Malt. Malt made must be entered with Officers of Excise once a Month, on Pain of £10. And Malsters using private Cisterns, *etc.* to forfeit £50, *etc. Stat. 8 & 9 W.3. c.22.; 13 & 14 W.3.*

Malsters concealing or conveying away Malt from the Sight of the Gauger, shall forfeit 10s. a Bushel; but Justices of Peace have Power to mitigate Penalties, so as they be not reduc'd to less than double Duty. *2 Ann. cap.2.*

And Malsters permitting Barley to be wetted on the Floor, or any where but in the Cistern entered, forfeit 2s. 6d. a Bushel. *Stat. 6 Geo.1. c.20.*

If any Malster, *etc.* fraudulently mix unmalted Corn with Malt; or Corn making into Malt of one wetting, with that of a former, *etc.* before put on the Kiln for drying, he shall forfeit 5s. *per* Bushel. *Stat. 1 Geo.1.; 2 Geo.2. c.1.*

Malt made for Exportation, is not liable to Duty; but must be enter'd, and kept separate, under the Penalty of £50 etc. *12 Geo.1.*

An Allowance is to be made Malsters for exporting Malt, by this Statute. *3 Geo 2. cap.7.*

The Forfeitures *supra* are leviable by Constables, *etc.*

Measures.

Constables, *etc.* are to examine if any Persons use Measures not agreeable to the Standard, by the Statute *22 Car.2.* And (by Virtue of a Warrant) to levy by Distress, the Forfeitures of such as sell Wine by Retail in Glass Bottles, or other Measures, not made of Pewter, and lawfully seal'd, (*viz.*) 50s. for every Offence, on Conviction before one or more Justices. *Stat. 2 W. & M. c.14.*

Persons beating or abusing Officers, *etc.* in the Execution of this Act, to be committed 'till the Sessions, and there fined £5.

Alehouse-Keepers, *etc.* are to sell their Ale by a full Ale Quart or Pint Measure, according to the Standard in the Exchequer, and mark'd, or forfeit a Sum not exceeding 40s. nor under 10s. leviable by Constables, *etc. Stat. 11 & 13 W.3. c.15.*

See more, Title *Weights* and *Measures.*

Militia.

Monies charged upon any Person by the Lord Lieutenant, or his Deputies, for the providing of Arms for Horse and Foot Soldiers in the Militia, are to be levied by Constables by Distress; and if no Distress is to be found, the Constables, by Warrant from the Lord Lieutenant, *etc.* may commit the Offender 'till Satisfaction be made.

Horsemen are to be provided with a Broad Sword, a Case of Pistols of twelve Inches long in the Barrel, a Carbine, with Belt and Bucket, Great Saddle, *etc.* And Foot Soldiers with a Musket five Foot long in the Barrel, the Gage of the Bore for Bullets of twelve to the Pound, with a Bayonet to fix in the Muzzle, a Cartouch-Box, and a Sword. *Stat. 1 Geo.1. c.11.*

Nightwalkers.

Constables are authorised by the Common Law to take up Night-walkers of ill Fame, end carry them before a Justice.

And common Night-walkers may be bound to the Good Behaviour; or be indicted before Justices of Peace, *etc.* So may Haunters of Bawdy-Houses. *1 Hawk. P. C.132.*

Norwich Stuffs. Vide *Cloth and Clothiers.*

Orchards.

Robbers of Orchards, Destroyers of Underwood, *etc.* shall be whipt by Constables, being order'd by a Justice of Peace's Warrant, for Default in making Satisfaction to the Party injur'd: The Satisfaction is at the Discretion of the Justice, and the Offender to pay a Sum not exceeding 10s. for the Poor. *Stat. 15 Car.2. c.2.*

See Title *Hedge breakers.*

Papists. See *Popish Recusants.*

Physicians.

Constables in the City of *London*, and within seven Miles, are to assist the

President of the College of Physicians, and such who shall have Authority from him, *etc.* to put the Laws in Execution concerning the said College. The Neglect is a Contempt to the King. *Stat. 14 & 15 H.8. c.5.*

And in *London, etc.* none shall practice Physick without License of the College, on pain of forfeiting £5 a Month, unless it be Persons having Knowledge in Herbs, *etc.* who may minister to outward Sores, and use Drinks for the Stone, Strangury, or Agues. *14 & 15 H.8.; 34 & 35 H.8. c.8.*

Four Physicians call'd Censors, to be yearly chosen by the College; who shall search Apothecaries Wares, and examine Medicines and burn or destroy those that are defective, *etc. Stat. 32 H.8. c.10.; 10 Geo.1.*

Plague.

Constables may command and oblige Persons infected with the Plague to keep within their Houses; and if after such Command, they wilfully go abroad, having any infectious Sores upon them, it is Felony; and if they have no Sores, they may be bound to the Good Behaviour, and punished as Vagabonds, by whipping, *etc. Stat. 1 Jac.1. cap.31.*

Constables neglecting to levy the Money assessed by Justices for Relief of poor Persons infected with the Plague, forfeit 10s. for every Offence. *Ibid. Stat.*

Justices of Peace, Mayors, *etc.* are to appoint Searchers, Watchmen, and Buriers of Persons infected, *etc.*

When the Plague is in any Country abroad, Ships are to perform *Quarentine*; and Persons quitting them before perform'd, shall forfeit £200. Goods after the Quarentine to be aired, and if infected burnt, *etc. Stat. 9 Ann. c.2.; 7 Geo.1. c.3.*

And the King by Proclamation, may prohibit Trade with Places infected: Landing Goods brought from thence is Felony. *Stat. 6 Geo.2. c.34.*

Popish Recusants.

In putting the Laws in Execution against Popish Recusants, Constables, *etc.* are concerned.

They may complain to a Justice of Persons suspected of Recusancy; and such Justice, on their Refusal of taking the Oath, may commit them till the next Assises or Sessions. *7 Jac.1. c.6.*

They are to present once a Year, to the Quarter-Sessions, those who absent themselves from Church for the Space of a Month; and the Names of their Children above nine Years of Age living with them, and such Servants as they retain. *Stat. 3 Jac.1. c.4.*

Neglecting, forfeit 20s. for every Default; And Popish Recusants forfeit £20 a Month for absenting from Church.

Constables are likewise to certify to the Quarter-Sessions, the Names of Popish Recusants convict, who within twenty Days after their Arrival at the Place of their Birth, (having no certain Settlement elsewhere) give in their Names; and the Parson of the Parish is to enter them in a Book for that Purpose. *Stat. 35 Eliz. c.2.*

Popish Recusants above the Age of Sixteen, are, within forty Days after their Conviction, to repair to their usual Dwellings, and not remove above five Miles from thence, on Pain of forfeiting all their Goods, *etc.* and if they have no certain Place of Residence, then they are to go to the Place of their Nativity, or where their

Parents dwell, and within twenty Days to give their Names in Writing, to the Minister, Constables, *etc. ut supra. Stat. Ibid.*

Papists are to register their Estates, on Pain of Forfeiture, *etc.* They are incapable to purchase Lands: And no Lands shall pass from Papists by Deed or Will, without Inrollment. *1 & 3 Geo.1.*

All Persons of the Age of Eighteen, to take the *Oaths*, or Register their Estates as Papists; but this is not to extend to Women, Persons having only an Estate in Reversion, or under £10 a Year, *etc.* And one Year's Rent of Lands to be forfeited, for Default of Registring. *Stat. 9 & 10 Geo.1.*

Post-Letters.

Sums under £5 due for Postage of Letters, are to be recover'd in the same Manner as small Tithes; by Complaint in Writing before two Justices, *etc.* and if the Party refuse to pay the Money awarded, in ten Days after Notice, a Constable, *etc.* by Warrant from the Justices, is to distrain his Goods, and the Distress may be sold in three Days. *Stat. 9 Ann. c.10.*

The Price of Postage is 3d. for a single Letter from any Place not distant above eighty Miles; for a double Letter 6d. and so proportionably for Packets. Packets of Writs, Deeds, *etc.* 12d. *per* Ounce: Single Letters above eighty Miles distant, 4d. double Letters 8d. single Letters to and from *Edinburgh* 6d. *etc.*

No Person but the Postmaster shall receive, take or carry Letters, *etc.* under the Penalty of £5. And Carriers, Stage Coachmen, *etc.* are not to carry any Letters, except such as concern Goods sent by them. *Stat. Ibid.*

Presentment.

Constables are to make Presentment on Oath at the Quarter-Sessions, and the Assizes, of all Things within their Knowledge against the peace, and relating to their Offices; as Affrays, Bloodsheds, Bridges out of Repair, Cottages erected contrary to Law, Drunkenness, Gaming-houses, Felonies, Forestallers, *etc.* Nusances, Disturbers of the Peace, Popish Recusants, Rescues, false Weights and Measures, *etc.* and generally all other Things mention'd in the particular Oath of Constables.

High Constables, by Virtue of a Warrant from Justices of Peace, issue their Precepts to Petty Constables, to make Enquiry and Presentment, *etc.* and they usually make their Returns, and bring them to a Justice to sign, and then carry them to the High Constable, who gives Oath that he had them from the Petty Constable. *Dalt.c.28.*

Form of a Constable's Presentment.

The Presentment of *A.B.* Constable of, *etc.* in the County of, *etc.* made at the General Quarter-Sessions of the Peace, held for the said County, the Day, *etc.*

The said A.B. says and presents upon his Oath, That C.D. of the Parish of, etc. in the County aforesaid, does at this Time keep, and has for the Space of one Month past, kept an unlawful Gaming-house in the said Parish of, etc. viz. he has permitted Servants, Apprentices, etc. to play at Cards, Dice, and other Games prohibited by Law, to the great Encouragement of Vice, and Disturbance of the Neighbourhood there.

The Compleat Parish Officer - Constables.

The said A.B. *likewise farther presents upon Oath, that* E.F. *of the said Parish of, etc. has lately carried out stinking Carcasses, and other Filth into the High Ways, which is a common Nusance to the Parish, and an Annoyance to Travellers. The said* A.B. *also presents* G.H. *to be a common Disturber of the Peace.*

Prisons.

The House of Correction, and the *Compters* of the Sheriffs of *London*, are the common Prisons for Offenders for the Breach of the Peace, *etc.*

To the last, Constables may convey Persons taken up by the Watch late at Night, and who are unruly or suspicious: But they ought to be careful who they send thither, for fear of Actions for false Imprisonment, and Prosecution for Damages.

Justices of Peace have Power to commit Criminals charged with small Offences either to the Common Gaol, or House of Correction. *Stat. 6 Geo.1. c.19.*

See Titles *Watch* and *Gaol.*

Prisoners.

Prisoners are to be relieved in Prison by our Laws and Statutes.

Justices of Peace in the Sessions, may Tax every Parish in the County, not exceeding a certain Sum yearly, for the Relief of poor Prisoners, leviable by Constables, *etc.* by *Stat. 43 Eliz. c.2.*

And by a late Statute, Persons charged in Execution for any Debt, not exceeding £100 on Petition to the Court whence the Process issued, with an Account of all their Estates and Effects upon Oath, may be discharged out of Prison, on assigning their Effects to the Creditors, unless they insist upon their being detained, and agree to pay them 2s. 4d. a Week, whilst in Prison. *Stat. 2 Geo.2. c.22.*

Prisoners in the Country are to have a Rule of Court to be brought to the next Assises for the County, at the Expence of 12d. a Mile, to be paid Officers out of their Effects, or of the County Stock, *etc.* And there they shall be discharged, by Order of the Judges, *etc. 3 Geo.2.*

Riots.

Sheriffs, Constables, *etc. ex officio*, are to suppress all Riots, and to commit the Offenders, and all such who break the Peace. *Stat. 17 R.2. c.8.*

And it is necessary to be observed, that when three or more Persons assemble together with an Intention of doing any unlawful Act, with Force and Violence, as to beat or wound a Man, pull down a House, Wall, or Hedge, or destroy any Park, Warren, *etc.* And if they only meet for such a Purpose, without putting their Designs in Practice; this is an *unlawful Assembly*: And if after such assembling, they move forwards to put their Projects in Execution, tho' they do not execute them, this is a *Rout*; and if they do perpetrate and execute what they intended, then it is adjudged a Riot: And going in Armour, or shewing any Intention of Violence, to the Terror of the King's Subjects, shall be deemed a *Riot. Pulton 24, etc.*

An Assembly of three or more who design no violent Act against the Peace, is not unlawful; and Assemblies on *Midsummer* and *May* Days, Bull baiting, Bear baiting, Football, and such Sports, Cudgel-playing, *etc.* Women meeting in Numbers, Stage-players, *etc.* are not forbidden by the Statutes; but causing a great Number of Stage-players to assemble is adjudged a Riot. *1 Roll. 9.*

If three, four, or more Persons, enter into Lands with Force, upon the Possession of another, tho' the Entry be lawful, yet it is a Riot; because Forcible Entries are prohibited by the Statute. *15 Ric.2. cap.2.; Dalt.297, etc.*

By the Statute *1 Geo.1. c.5.* if twelve or more unlawfully and riotously assemble, a Justice of Peace, Sheriff, Mayor, or other Head Officer of any Town Corporate, on Notice of such Assembly, shall come as near them as he can with Safety, and make the following Proclamation:

Our Sovereign Lord the King charges and commands all Persons assembled immediately to disperse themselves, and peaceably depart to their Habitations or lawful Business, on Pain of Imprisonment,. or the Penalties inflicted by the Act made in the First Year of the Reign of King George I. *for preventing Tumults and riotous Assemblies.* God save the King.

If the Rioters do not disperse within an Hour after this Proclamation made; or if they obstruct or hinder the Proclamation, or hurt him who makes it, it is Felony without Benefit of Clergy; and High Constables, Petty Constables, and Persons assisting may seize them, and carry them before a Justice; and if any of the Rioters are killed, he who killed them is indemnified.

Demolishing a Meeting-House, Dwelling-House, Barn, Stable, *etc.* is made Felony; and the Town or Hundred shall yield Damages to repair.

Persons going abroad arm'd in Disguises, robbing Forests, Parks, Fish-ponds, or setting Fire to any House, shooting at Persons, sending threatning Letters demanding Money, killing or maiming Cattle, cutting down Trees in any Avenue, Garden, *etc.* are guilty of Felony, by the Statute *9 Geo.1. c.23.*

Robbery.

Robbery is a felonious Taking away of Money or Goods from the Person of another, in a violent Manner.

Where Damages are recovered against a Hundred for a Robbery committed on the Highway, and two Justices have set a Tax upon the several Parishes in the Hundred; the Constables in every Parish are to tax particularly every Inhabitant of those Parishes, and levy the same by Distress, *etc. Stat. 27 Eliz. cap.13.*

The Hundred is chargeable where a Robbery is committed in the Day-time, of any Day, except *Sunday.* But no Hundred shall be chargeable if any one of the Malefactors is apprehended in forty Days; or when the Action is not commenced within a Year. *Ibid. Stat.*

A Reward of £40 is ordered by Statute for apprehending a Robber on the Highway; and the Apprehenders to have likewise the Horses, Arms, *etc.* of Robbers. *4 & 5 W. & M.*

See *Hue and Cry.*

Rogues.

Constables are to whip wandering Rogues, Vagabonds, *etc.* by stripping them naked from the Middle upwards, and causing them to be lashed until their Bodies be bloody, in the Presence of the Minister of the Parish, or some other Inhabitants; and then to send them away to the Place of their Birth, *etc.* Not endeavouring to seize Rogues, or punish them, forfeit 10s.

Persons running away from their Families, and leaving a Charge to the Parish, are to be punished as *incorrigible Rogues*; and if any threaten so to do, without giving Security to the Parish, he may be committed to the House of Correction. *Dalt.211.*

And *Note*; Those Rogues are looked upon incorrigible, as appear dangerous to the inferior Sort of People; threatning or offering any Violence to them, or that will not reform after being once whipped, *etc.* And by the Statute *1 Jac.1. c.7.* they were to be punished by burning on the left Shoulder the first Time; and offending again it was declared Felony. But this Statute is repealed; and by the Stat. *12 Ann.* an incorrigible Rogue is to be whipped three Market-Days in some Market-Town, and kept at hard Labour so long as the Justices shall think fit: Though if he makes his Escape, it is Felony by this Act.

Vide more Title *Vagrants.*

Sabbath. See *Sunday.*

Servants.

The Statute *5 Eliz. cap.4.* directs Testimonials to be given by Mayors of Towns, Constables, and two Householders, to Servants quitting their Services. A Servant not producing a Testimonial to the chief Officer in a Corporation, or to the Constable, Minister, or Church-wardens where he designs to dwell, may be imprisoned 'till he can get one; and if he do not procure one in one and twenty Days, he is to be whipp'd and punish'd as a Vagabond; and Masters retaining a Servant without such Testimonial, forfeit £5.

A Testimonial for a Servant.

I A.B. of, etc. in the County of, etc. do hereby license my Servant C.D. to depart from my Service, he having served me faithfully; and I do declare the said C.D. is at full Liberty to serve any other Master elsewhere, according to the Statute in that Case made and provided. Witness my Hand, etc. this Day, etc. A.B.

We do hereby allow of the above License and Testimonial.

E. F. *Constable of, etc. aforesaid.* G. H. and J.K.- *Householders there*

This good Statute is of late very little regarded.

See more, Title *Servants* under the Head *Church-wardens*, and *Overseers of the Poor*.

Shoemakers.

Master and Wardens of the Shoemakers Company in *London*, and Mayors, *etc.* shall appoint Searchers and Sealers of Leather; Leather not sufficiently tanned, to be forfeited; and being sold before searched and sealed, incurs the Penalty of 6s. 8d. Also Shoemakers are to make their Shoes of sufficient Stuff, on Pain of 3s. 4d. to be levied by Constables, by Warrant from Justices, *etc. Stat. 1 Jac.1. c.22.; 13 & 14 Car.2.*

If any Journeyman Shoemaker, within *London* or the Bills of Mortality, purloin, imbezil, sell, or pawn any Materials for making of Shoes, *etc.* he shall be ordered by a Justice to make Satisfaction, or to be whipt.

Justices of Peace may grant Warrants to Constables to search after such Goods, in the Houses of Persons suspected to have the same. *Stat. 9 Geo.1. c.27.*

Soldiers.

Constables, Tithingmen, *etc.* are to quarter Soldiers in Inns, Livery-Stables, Ale-houses, Victualling-Houses, and Houses selling Brandy, *etc.* (Distillers and private Houses excepted.) *Stat. 1 Geo.1. c.3.*

Refusing to billet Soldiers, shall be fined not exceeding 40s. nor less than 10s. And if they receive any Reward to excuse Quarterage; or if Victuallers refuse Soldiers quarter'd, shall forfeit not under 40s. nor above £5. *1 Geo.1. c.34.; 7 Geo.1. c.6.; 1 Geo.2.*

If any Soldiers shall be billeted on private Houses, without the Owner's Consent, he may have his Remedy at Law; and any military Officer quartering Soldiers otherwise than as directed by Statute, or abusing the Constable, *etc.* shall be cashiered. Any Justice of Peace may command Constables, *etc.* to give an Account in writing of the Number of Officers and Soldiers billeted by them, with the Names of the Persons on whom billeted, and their Streets, Signs, *etc.* to prevent Abuses in the Quartering of Soldiers.

Officers Civil or Military are not to Quarter the Wives, Children, or Servants of Officers or Soldiers in any House without the Consent of the Owner, on Pain of being Cashiered, if an Officer of the Army; and of forfeiting 20s. if a Constable, *etc.* leviable by Warrant of the next Justice of the Peace. *3 Geo.2. c.2.*

Soldiers suspected of Desertion, to be taken up by Constables, *etc.* and 20s. Reward is given for apprehending them: Persons concealing Deserters, buying their Clothes, *etc.* to forfeit £5. And persuading and procuring Soldiers to desert, incurs a Penalty of £40.

During the late War with *France*, a Constable had Power to press able-bodied Men, having no lawful Employment, or visible Means of Maintenance, by Virtue of a Warrant from three Justices; and to bring them before the said Justices, who were to deliver them to some of his Majesty's Officers appointed to recruit the Army, and such Officers were to pay each Soldier 20s. and the Constable was to have 10s. for every Man: If the Soldier listed himself voluntarily, he was advanced 40s. *Stat. 2 & 3 Ann.* And these Encouragements were doubled by subsequent Acts.

By *11 & 12 W.3.* Lewd and disorderly Servants, Vagabonds, and sturdy Beggars, were to be sent to serve his Majesty at Sea, by Warrant from a Justice directed to the Constable, *etc.*

Constables and Church-wardens, are to levy by Distress, Money rated on Persons for Relief of poor maimed Soldiers and Mariners, and pay it to the High Constable. *Stat. 43 Eliz.*

Sunday.

Search is usually made on a Sunday, by Constables and other Parish-Officers, after such as prophane the Sabbath, *etc.*

Persons who resort to Wrestling, Bowling, Dancing, or any Sport, on a Sunday, forfeit 5s. if above fourteen Years of Age, and 1s. if under, levied by Constables by Warrant of one Justice; and Constables, Church-wardens, *etc.* are to levy the Penalty of 3s. 4d. of such as use Bull-baiting, Games or Plays, on a Sunday, for the Use of the Poor, by Distress, for Want whereof the Offenders shall be set in the Stocks three Hours. *Stat. 1 Car.1. cap.1.*

If any Person doth any worldly Labour on a Sunday, (except Works of Necessity) he shall forfeit 5s. And crying or exposing to Sale any Wares, unless it be Milk and Mackarel, incurs a Forfeiture of the Wares to the Poor. Butchers killing or selling Victuals, are liable to a Penalty of 6s. 8d. Carriers or Drovers, *etc.* travelling, shall forfeit 20s. and Persons using Boats, *etc.* on a Sunday, (not allowed by a Justice of Peace) forfeit 5s. *Stat. 29 Car.2. c.7.*

If any Persons shall serve any Warrant, Process, *etc.* on Sundays, (except in Cases of Treason, Felony, or Breach of the Peace) they shall answer Damages as if done without Warrant, for false Imprisonment, and the Service be void. *29 Car.2. c.7.*

If any one disturb a Minister in Preaching, Praying, or administring the Sacraments, Constables may apprehend him and carry him before a Justice, *etc. 1 Mar.*

See the general Head *Church-wardens.*

Supersedeas.

If a Constable have a Warrant to execute for Sureties of the Peace; and afterwards having a *Supersedeas* from the Court of Chancery, or from another Justice, *etc.* to discharge the Sureties, he still insists upon having the Party find Sureties, and he refuse, and is detained, it is false Imprisonment in the Constable. *Dalt. Nat. Br.524.*

A *Supersedeas* is as good Cause to discharge a Person, as the first Warrant or Process is to arrest him. *2 Cro.379.*

Swearing.

There are several good Laws made for the Prevention and Punishment of this Crime.

And Constables are to levy the Penalties on Offenders, which are 1s. for a Servant, Labourer, *etc.* and 2s. for every other Person, to the Poor; and double for the second Offence, and treble for the Third, to be levied by Warrant of one Justice, *etc. Stat. 6 & 7 W. & M. c.11.*

If there be no Distress for levying the Penalty for prophane Swearing, the Offender is to be set in the Stocks one Hour for the first Offence, and two Hours for further Offences, if above sixteen Years of Age; and if under, to be whipp'd.

Taylors.

Taylors giving greater Wages than the Statute allows, shall forfeit £5. And their Journeymen accepting thereof, or refusing to work for Wages allow'd, shall be sent to the House of Correction for two Months.

And Masters not paying lawful Wages, it shall be levied by Distress, *etc.* by Constables, by Virtue of Justice of Peace's Warrant. *Stat. 7 Geo.1. c.13.*

See *Buttons.*

Tithes.

In *London* the Sums of Money ordered in Lieu of Tithes, are to be paid quarterly to the Parsons, *etc.* and upon Refusal to pay the same, the Lord Mayor may grant Warrants for the Collector, with the Assistance of a Constable, to levy it by Distress and Sale of Goods. *Stat. 22 & 23 Car.2. c.15.*

Constables and Headboroughs, by Virtue of a Warrant from two Justices, are to levy Money adjudged for refusing the Payment of small Tithes, by Distress, and Sale in three Days; and if they retain the Charges for making the Distress, two Justices of Peace have Power to summon the Party, hear the Complaint by

The Compleat Parish Officer - Constables.

Witnesses on Oath, and give Judgment by making an Allowance for the Tithes, and ordering Costs not exceeding 10s. *Stat. 7 & 8 W.3.* and *3 & 4 Ann.* The Tithes are to be under 40s. *per Ann.* And Tithes due from Quakers, under £10, are thus recoverable. But this Remedy is extended to the Recovery of any Tithes, or Church-Rates due from Quakers, by *1 Geo.1. cap.7.*

Tobacco.

Constables, *etc.* upon Information of Tobacco, set, sown or planted, in any Ground (except Physick Gardens,) are to destroy the same within fourteen Days after receiving a Warrant from two Justices of the Peace to that Purpose, on Pain of forfeiting 5s. for every Rod unconsumed. *Stat. 22 & 23 Car.2. cap.26.*

Persons resisting the Officers shall forfeit £5 to be levied by Distress and Sale, or be committed for three Months; and Persons refusing to assist the Constable forfeit 5s. or to be committed for a Week.

Constables, upon Warrant, are to make a Search, and present Offences of planting Tobacco, *etc.* at the next Quarter-Sessions: And those that plant it, are liable to the Penalty of £10 for every Rod of Ground so planted in *England. Stat. 17 Car.2. c.7.; 22 & 23 Car.2.*

Cutting Walnut-Tree Leaves, and other Leaves, or Colouring them to resemble Tobacco; or selling them mixed with Tobacco, incurs a Forfeiture of 5s. *per* Pound. *1 Geo.1. c.46.*

Vagrants.

The Particulars relating to Constables in the late vagrant Act, for reducing all the Laws on that Subject into one, are as follow.

Constables, or other Inhabitants, are to apprehend Vagrants, and carry them before a Justice of Peace: And wandering Patent-Gatherers, and Collectors for Prisons, Fencers, Bear-wards, common Players of Interludes, Juglers, Gypsies, or Persons wandering in their Habit or Form; Pretenders to Physiognomy, Fortune-Tellers, Users of subtle Craft, or unlawful Games; able-bodied Persons, who run away and leave their Wives or Children to the Parish; Persons refusing to work for common Wages, not having otherwise to maintain them; and other idle Persons wandering abroad and begging (except Soldiers, Mariners, *etc.* licensed by a Testimonial from Justices) are adjudged Vagrants. *Stat. 12 Ann. Sess. 2. c.23.*

Constables, or Officers neglecting to apprehend them, is a Breach of Duty; and any other Inhabitants refusing to apprehend Vagrants, being charged by a Justice, forfeit 10s. to the Poor, to be levied by Distress.

As a Reward for Apprehension, a Justice of Peace may by his Warrant order the Constable or other Officer where a Vagabond was found begging unapprehended, to pay 2s. to the Person apprehending, and a Recompence for Trouble and Loss of Time is to be satisfied.

Constables in their several Divisions are to make a general privy Search for Rogues, Vagabonds, *etc.* before the Quarter-Sessions, by Virtue of a Warrant from Justices of Peace, and to carry such as they find before the said Justices, *etc.*

Where any Person is apprehended and brought before a Justice of Peace, he is to examine of his Condition and Circumstances, and Place of Abode or Birth, upon Oath as well of the Party as of any other; the Substance of which is to be transmitted to the Quarter-Sessions to be recorded: If it appear such Person has obtained any legal Settlement, then he is to be sent to such Place; if it cannot be found he hath gain'd any legal Settlement since his Birth, then the Justice or Justices are by Pass under Hand and Seal, (directed to the Constables where the Vagabond was apprehended) to cause such Person to be conveyed to the Place of Birth; or if he be under the Age of fourteen, and have Father or Mother living, to the Abode of such Father or Mother; and if that be not known, to the Parish or Place where found last begging, and passed unapprehended, and there delivered to the Constable.

Persons refusing to be examined upon Oath, or giving a false Account of themselves, their Birth, Settlements, *etc.* shall be deemed incorrigible Rogues.

The Justices who make the Pass, shall at the same Time give the Constable a Certificate, ascertaining how the Vagrant is to be convey'd, either by Horse, or on Foot, and to what Place, and in what Time, and the Allowance to be made to the Officer: Constables, *etc.* Counterfeiting the Certificate, altering the Sum, *etc.* forfeit £20 one Moiety to the Poor, the other to the Informer.

The Constable is to pursue the Directions in the Pass and Certificate, and pass the Vagrant the direct Way to the Place where he is ordered to be sent, if it is in the same County where he is apprehended; if not, then to the first Town of the next County nam'd in the Pass or Certificate, and deliver him to the Constable or Headborough there; together with the Pass, taking a Receipt of the Delivery upon the Back of the Certificate.

Such next Constable or Headborough must forthwith carry the Vagrant before a Justice, *etc.* to be stript and whipt, or be sent to the House of Correction for two or three Days; from whence he is to be conveyed with the aforesaid Pass, but with a new Certificate, to the next County, and so from County to County to the Place first ordered.

A Justice may examine a Constable upon Oath touching such Conveying; and if he refuses to be sworn, or neglects his Duty in any Thing, then he is to lose the Sum allowed by the Certificate.

When a Petty Constable has convey'd the Vagrant to the Place ordered by the Pass, on his bringing to the High Constable such Certificate as aforesaid, with the Receipt from the Constable or other Officer to whom the Vagrant was delivered, the Chief Constable shall pay such Petty Constable the Allowance ascertained in the Certificate, and no more, taking the said Certificate and his Receipt, which is to be allowed the Chief Constable by the Treasurer of the County.

Justices in Sessions are to appoint Allowances for passing Vagrants at so much a Mile, or otherwise; and make Orders for raising Money for that Purpose, to be paid quarterly to the High Constables. And Rates for reconveying, being likewise appointed by Justices of Peace in the Sessions, the Constable must make Oath before a Justice of what Expences he is at in reconveying Vagrants to *Ireland*, or any Place abroad; whereupon the Justice is to direct the Payment by an Order under Hand and Seal.

Vagabonds brought from *Ireland*, and apprehended here begging, may be put on Board any Vessel in Order to be reconveyed: And a Master of a Ship bringing over a

Vagrant from any of the Plantations, being a Native thereof, shall forfeit £5 for every Vagabond found begging here.

A Constable where such a Vagrant is found begging, may cause him to be whipped, and afterwards put on Board any other Vessel in Order to be sent back again; paying so much *per* Head, as the Sessions shall appoint, and the Master must give a Receipt on the Back of the Justice's Warrant for the Money paid him by the Constable for Transportation.

A Master of a Ship refusing to take Vagrants on Board, forfeits £5 to the Use of the Poor.

Vagrants having no legal Settlement, or who have been common Beggars for two Years, and incorrigible Rogues, may be bound Apprentice for Seven Years, and sent to the Plantations.

A Constable, on Complaint of Inhabitants, is to remove loose, idle and disorderly Persons, Blind, Lame, *etc.* from begging in the Streets and Highways; and on their Refusal to be gone, if they beg a second Time, may cause them to be whipt.

Constables, *etc.* neglecting or refusing so to do, shall forfeit 10s. for every Offence: And failing in their Duties in apprehending and conveying Vagrants; or any Person disturbing them in the Execution of their Office, rescuing Vagrants, *etc.* incurs a Forfeiture of 20s. for the Use of the Poor, to be levied by Distress.

Furious Lunaticks wandering, may be apprehended and passed to their legal Place of Settlement in the same Manner as Vagrants are to be sent, (whipping excepted) but the Expence is to be defrayed out of their Estates by Order of Justices, if they have any; and if they have none, the Charges to be raised by such Ways as Monies are raised for the Poor.

At *Easter* Quarter-Sessions yearly, the Justices ascertain and set down the several Rates that shall, for the Year ensuing, be allowed for maintaining, conveying and carrying of Vagrants. And Copies are to be delivered to the Justices, by the Clerk of the Peace. These Rates have been settled at 6d. *per* Mile for a Carriage, and 1d. *per* Mile for a Horse; besides reasonable Expences allow'd Constables on the Road.

By the Statute *13 & 14 Car.2. c.12.* Constables, *etc.* and other Inhabitants, may tax Persons chargeable to reimburse their Charges for conveying Vagabonds, *etc.* to the House of Correction, and for other Parish-Charges: And the Persons to be tax'd are every Inhabitant of the Parish, *viz.* the Parson, Vicar, and all Occupiers of Houses, Lands, Tithes and Woods; but a Landlord is not to be tax'd in Respect of his Rent: And this Tax or Rate must be confirm'd under the Hands and Seals of two Justices.

There are some *Law Cases* relating to Vagrants: Whoever is able to work, but will not, and wanders abroad, having nothing to subsist on but by his Labour, is a Vagrant Rogue. *Dalt.308.*

Although a Man have a certain Habitation, yet if he wander out of his own Parish, begging, or otherwise misordering himself, he may be punish'd as a Vagrant. *2 Roll. Rep.172.*

No one is to be put out of the Town where he dwelleth. nor to be sent to the

Place of his Birth or Habitation, but only a Vagrant Rogue; such as wanders abroad in the Country, and not those that are Vagabonds, and beg in the same Town where they dwell. *2 Salk.526.*

A Pass of a Vagrant to his Place of Birth.

Whereas J.B. being about the Age of, *etc.* was apprehended in the Parish of, *etc.* aforesaid, there wandering and begging, and committing other Acts of Vagrancy, and brought before me *J.S.* Esq. one of his Majesty's Justices of Peace, for the County aforesaid; and upon Examination of the said *J.B.* and of, *etc.* taken upon Oath, it doth appear that the said *J.B.* was born at, *etc.* in the County of, *etc.* and that the said *J.B.* hath not obtained any legal Settlement elsewhere: *These are therefore* to command and require you to convey the said *J.B.* the next direct Way to the Parish of, *etc.* and there deliver him to the Constable, *etc.* that being the first Town or Parish in the next County or Precinct, through which he ought to pass to the said Parish of, *etc.* to be thence convey'd on according to the Direction of the late Act of Parliament, to the said Parish of, *etc.* in the County of, *etc.* aforesaid. And I do hereby allow the Space of three Days for his passing to the said Parish of, *etc. Given, etc.*

A Receipt from the next Constable, on Delivery of a Vagrant.

I *A.B.* Constable of, *etc.* in the County of, *etc.* do hereby acknowledge that I have received this Day, *etc.* of and from *C.D.* Constable of, *etc.* in the County of, *etc. E.F.* and *G.H.* Vagrants, by the said *C.D.* brought hither in their Way to, *etc.* by Virtue of a Pass granted by, *etc. Witness my Hand, etc.*

Watch.

Constables of Towns are to cause Night-Watches to be set from Sun-set to Sun-rising, with four Men or more, (in a City six Men at every Gate) who must be able Persons, Inhabitants of the Place, and watch by Turns. *Stat. Winchester c.4.*

Persons refusing to serve on the Watch, on Complaint to a Justice of Peace, he may compel them, or bind them to the Good Behaviour; and some Authors are of Opinion, that the Constable has Power to set the Party in the Stocks for Contempt: But this seems rather to be when a Watchman appointed is not orderly in the doing of his Duty. *Dalt.240.*

These Watchmen are to apprehend Night-Walkers, Vagabonds, Persons going armed, *etc.* and they may arrest Strangers in the Night, and examine them; and if they find Cause of Suspicion, secure them till the Morning; and whether they be Horsemen or Footmen, or Drivers of Cattle, Carriages, or that shall carry Burdens, the Watch may stay them 'till the Morning, unless they can render a good Account of themselves, their Company, and Carriage, *etc. Dalt.240.* Constables shall be aiding and assisting to the Watch; and the Watchmen are to obey their Orders, in conveying Offenders to the Counter, *etc.*

If any will not obey the Arrest, the Watch may make Hue and Cry upon them; and for such Arrest of a Stranger, (especially one suspected) none is liable to Punishment.

Weights and Measures.

There is to be one Measure, *etc.* throughout the Kingdom. *Magn. Chart. 9 H.3.*

Every City, Borough and Town, is to have a common Ballance to weigh Goods bought and sold, with common Weights seal'd, in the Keeping of the Head Officer or Constable there; otherwise the City forfeits £10 the Borough £4 and the Town 40s. to the King. *Stat. 8 H.6. c.5.*

At this Ballance all the Inhabitants of the City, Borough, *etc.* may weigh *gratis;* but Foreigners shall, for every Draught under forty Pounds, pay a Farthing; for a Draught between forty Pounds, and a Hundred an Half-penny; and above a hundred Pounds a Penny, *etc. Stat. Ibid.*

In every City, Borough and Market-Town, shall be a common Bushel seal'd, according to the Standard, in like Manner as common Ballance, on Pain as in the Statute *8 H.6.* And a Bushel shall contain eight Gallons of Wheat, every Gallon eight Pounds, each Pound twelve Ounces, and every Ounce twenty Penny Weights or Sterlings. *Stat. 11 H.6. c.8.; 12 H.7. c.5.*

Measures and Weights of Brass, are to be sent to every City and Borough; and Mayors or Chief Officers in Cities and Boroughs, shall have a special Mark for Sealing of Weights and Measures, and take one Penny for sealing a Bushel, and a Half-penny for every other Measure, and for every Hundred-weight a Penny, Half a Hundred a Half-penny, every less Weight a Farthing; and if they refuse or delay to seal, shall forfeit 40s. Sealing any Weight or Measure not agreeable to the Standard; or suffering Persons to sell or buy by other Measures, *etc.* incurs a Forfeiture of £5. *7 H.7. c.4.*

Mayors, *etc.* shall view all Measures and Weights, once a Year; break or burn those which are defective, and inflict a Penalty of 6s. 8d. on Offenders. *Stat. 11 Hen.7. c.4.*

Whosoever shall buy or sell by false Weights or Measures, shall forfeit 5s. leviable by Distress, *etc.* by Statute *17 Car.1. c.19.*

Also an Indictment will lie for selling by false Weights and Measures, it being an Offence at Common Law as well as by Statute.

Constables may search and examine if any Persons use other Measures than such as are *Winchester* Measure, and agreeable to the Standard in the Exchequer, and sealed, *etc.* and if they find any unseal'd, they may break them, and present the Offenders at the next Quarter-Sessions. *Stat. 22 Car.2. c.8.*

Persons selling Corn or Salt by any Bushel or Measure not according to the Standard; and struck even with the Brim, forfeit 40s. and the Corn, *etc. Stat. 22 Car.2.*

Bakers selling their Bread under Weight, *etc.* vide *Bakers.*

Wrecks.

Constables are to call Assistance, by Command of Justices, and endeavour to preserve Ships in Danger of a Wreck, near the Sea-Coasts; and Officers of Men of War, and other Ships, are to be aiding, *etc.* under the Penalty of £100. *Stat. 12 Ann. c.18.*

No Person shall enter any such Ship without Leave from the Commander, Constable *etc.* Persons carrying away Goods from Ships in Distress, are liable to pay treble Value; but the Persons assisting shall be allow'd a reasonable Reward for Salvage, *etc. Stat. Ibid.*

By the Statute *3 Ed.1.* where a Man or any living Creature escapes alive out of a

Ship cast away, the same shall not be adjudg'd a Wreck; but the Goods shall be sav'd and kept by the Sheriff a Year and a Day for the Owner, *etc.*

Warrants.

A Constable is not to dispute a Justice of Peace's Warrant; but is to execute the same with all convenient Speed; and if the Justice exceeds his Authority, (that is if he grants a Warrant to arrest a Person for Breach of the Peace, without Cause, *etc.*) the Constable is excused; but if a Justice issues a Warrant to be executed out of his Jurisdiction, where he has no Authority, and he is not a proper Judge, the Constable will be punished if he executes it. *14 H.8. c.16.; Lamb.67.; Dalt.465.*

And it is the same if the Constable executes a Warrant, that has apparent Mistakes in the Penalty required to be levied; or out of his Precinct. *Dalt.464.*

But it is said if a Warrant is directed to a Constable by Name, commanding him to execute it, tho' he is not compellable to go out of his Parish, yet he may if he will, and shall be justified by the Warrant in so doing; but if it is directed to all Constables generally, and to none in particular by Name, there a Constable out of the Precinct cannot execute it. *Dalt.1.; Salk.175.*

If a Warrant be general, *etc.* to bring an Offender before the Justice who grants it, or any other Justice, *etc.* the Constable may carry the Party before any Magistrate, at his Election; *5 Rep. Foster's* Case. But where the Warrant directs the Bringing the Party before the Justice that granted it, the Constable must carry him before that Justice, and no other.

A Constable or any sworn Officer, need not shew his Warrant when he comes to serve it; acquainting the Person with the Contents is sufficient: And if any Officer say, *I arrest you in the King's Name,* tho' he be no sworn Officer, the Party must obey at his Peril, he having a lawful Warrant. If the Officer is resisted or assaulted in executing the Warrant, he may justify the Beating and Wounding, *etc. 9 Co.69.*

In Cases of Treason, Felony, or Breach of the Peace, where the King is Party, a Constable may, by Warrant from a Justice of Peace, break open a House to take a Criminal; but he ought first to demand the Opening of the Doors, and to signify to the Person the Cause of his coming. *Cromp.171.*

A Constable may not retake an Offender after he has arrested him, and let him go upon his Promise to return and appear before a Justice, by Virtue of his first Warrant. And if a Constable apprehend a Person without a Warrant, and obtain one afterwards, it is false Imprisonment; also if a Warrant is granted against a particular Person by Name, and he apprehends another of the same Name, such Taking is wrongful; but if there are two Persons of one Name, and the same Additions, and the Constable arrests a wrong Person, it is no false Imprisonment. *Dyer 244.; Dalt.484.*

A Justice's Warrant ought to express the Cause of its being granted. No Justice or Justices of Peace can make a Warrant upon a bare Surmise, to break any Man's House to search for a Felon or stolen Goods; there must be a Felony actually committed, and sworn to, whereon to ground their Warrant. A general Warrant to search after Felons, *etc.* hath been held illegal. *2 Hawk.13.* but see *Dalt.114.*

If any Person throw into the Dirt, tread under Foot, or shew any other Contempt to a Justice of Peace's lawful Warrant, he shall be bound to the Good Behaviour, and may be indicted and fined. *Cromp.149.*

A Justice of Peace's Warrant to a High Constable, to issue his Precept to Petty Constables, to make Presentment of Offences at the Quarter-Sessions.

To A.B. *Constable of the Hundred of, etc.*

Berks, ss. THESE are, in his Majesty's Name, to command you to issue your Precepts to the several Petty Constables in all and every the Precincts within your Hundred, requiring them to make true and faithful Presentment at the next General Quarter-Sessions of the Peace to be holden for this County, at, *etc.* on, *etc.* of all and every the Offences committed in their several Limits, which they are by their Oaths oblig'd to enquire into, *viz.* Affrays, Bloodsheds, *etc.* [*Here set forth the Particulars*] and that you do then and there appear at the said Quarter-Sessions, to make Return of this Warrant, and do herein as the Acts of Parliament direct; hereof fail not at your Peril. *Given* under our Hands this Day, *etc. Anno Dom'*, *etc.*

The High Constable's Precept to Petty Constables to make such Presentment.

Berks, ss. By Virtue of a Warrant to me directed from *A.B.*; *C.D. etc.* Esqs; Justices of the Peace within the County aforesaid; *These* are to charge and require you to make your personal Appearance at the General Quarter-Sessions of the Peace, to be holden at, *etc.* on, *etc.* next, for this County, and bring with you thither, fairly written, all your Presentments of Treasons, Felonies, Murders, Robberies, Thefts, Riots, Routs, Bloodsheds, Rescues, Hues and Cries not prosecuted, Gaming-houses, Drunkenness, Forestallers, Cottages erected against the Statute, Bridges and Highways out of Repair, common Nusances, Bawdy-houses, Disturbers of the Peace, Alehouse-keepers unlicensed, and Disorders in Ale-houses, false Weights and Measures, Watches and Wards not kept, and generally all Manner of Trespasses and Offences whatsoever, inquirable by you, and committed within your Precincts, to the End the Offenders may be proceeded against according to Law. *Given* under my Hand, *etc.*

See the Form of *Presentments of Constables*, under Title *Presentment.*

The High Constable's Warrant to make a privy Search.

By Virtue of a Warrant to me directed from *A.B.* and *C.D.* Esqrs; two of his Majesty's Justices of the Peace for this County, acting within the Hundred of, *etc.* aforesaid; *These* are to command you to make diligent Search and Enquiry within your Precincts, upon *Monday* next in the Night-time, after Rogues, Vagabonds, and sturdy Beggars, and all such Persons as are suspected to keep Bawdy-houses, and the Frequenters thereof, and also all Disturbers of the Peace, *etc.* and to apprehend them, and bring them before, *etc.* upon *Tuesday* next by Ten of the Clock in the Forenoon; to be dealt with according to Law: Hereof fail not. Dated, *etc.*

A High Constable's Precept to Petty Constables, to prepare Lists of Jurors.

By Virtue of a Warrant from, *etc.* Justices of Peace, at the General Quarter-Sessions held for the County aforesaid, at, *etc.* on, *etc.* last past: *These* are to require you to make and prepare a sufficient List of Persons qualified to serve on Juries, *viz.* of the Names and Places of Habitation of Persons between the Age of Twenty one and Seventy, having £80 *per Ann.* to serve on the Grand Jury; and of those as have £10 *per Ann.* Freehold, to serve on the Petty Jury, (Aliens, Infants,

Apothecaries, Clergymen, Conspirators, or Persons attainted excepted) and that you do make a Return of the said List at the next General Quarter-Sessions (*Michaelmas*) to be held for this County. *Given, etc.*

A Warrant from a High Constable to a Petty Constable to levy Gaol-Money.

By Virtue of a Warrant to me directed by his Majesty's Justices of the Peace assembled at the General Quarter-Sessions held, *etc.* for this County; I do hereby require you to levy of all and every the Inhabitants in your Parish, the Sum of, *etc.* towards the Reparation of the County-Gaol, which said Sum is thought fit by the Justices aforesaid, to be raised in your Parish, by an equal Taxation; and if any Person shall refuse to pay his or their Parts of the said Tax, four Days after demanded, that then you do levy the same by Distress and Sale, *etc.* within a further Space of four Days, returning the Overplus, after deducting the Charges of the Distress, to the Owner. *Given, etc.*

High Constable's Warrant to levy Money for Repair of Bridges.

By Virtue of a Warrant to me directed by his Majesty's Justices of the Peace, *etc.* (*ut supra*) *These* are to require you to levy the Sum of, *etc.* of all and every the Inhabitants in your Parish, by an equal Assessment, towards the Repairs of the County Bridges; and that you do pay the same to me on, *etc.* next at, *etc.* in order to my carrying and accounting for the same to the Quarter-Sessions. *Given, etc.*

A Receipt for Money for passing Vagrants.

Receiv'd this Day, *etc.* of *A.B.* High Constable of the Hundred of, *etc.* the Sum of, *etc.* for conveying *C.D.* a Vagrant, to the Town of, *etc.* being the Sum ascertain'd in the Justice's Certificate within mention'd. *Witness* my Hand, this, *etc.*

E. F. Petty Constable of, etc.

Where there are different Tithings, Hundreds and Counties, there must be different Constables, although in the same Parish, and they must Account for their Offices before other Justices, *etc.* But though a Parish be in several Counties, the Authority of Church-wardens is the same in every Part of it, as if all were in one County; for they must follow the Ecclesiastical Jurisdiction, which is into Dioceses, Archdeaconries, *etc.*

If an Action be brought against a Constable, Church-warden, *etc.* for any Thing done in the Execution of their Offices, they may in all Cases plead the General Issue, and give the special Matter in Evidence; and if the Plaintiff is nonsuited, discontinue, or a Verdict be for the Defendant, he shall have double Costs. *Stat.* 7 *Jac.*1.; 25 *Jac.* c.12.

OF CHURCH-WARDENS AND OVERSEERS OF THE POOR,

Their Duties and Offices, *etc.* in all Cases.

Church-wardens are very ancient Officers, and by the Common Law they are in the Nature of a Corporation to take Care of the Goods of the Church; the Property whereof is in them; but they have nothing to do with the Lands.

They are elected by the Canon, *1 Jac.1.* by the Minister and Parishioners, or by their joint Consent, in *Easter* Week, yearly; and if they happen to disagree, then the Minister is to chuse one, and the Parishioners another, unless there be a Custom to the contrary, which must be observed. *2 Roll. Abr.287.*

When a Church-warden is chosen by Virtue of any particular Custom, the Archdeacon is to swear him, though the Election be against the Canon; and if he refuses, a *Mandamus* lies to compel him. *3 Cro.551.*

An Archdeacon refusing one that is chosen, and appointing another against the Consent of the Parish, the Court of King's Bench will issue out a special Writ to the Bishop to swear him; and a Church-warden being a temporal Officer entrusted with the Parish Goods, the Parishioners may chuse and put in Trust whom they think fit. *1 Vent.266.*

The Oath of Church-warden.

You shall swear truly and faithfully to execute the Office of a Church-warden within your Parish, according to the best of your Skill and Knowledge; and present such Things and Persons as to your Knowledge are presentable, by the Laws Ecclesiastical of this Realm. So help you God.

The Office of Church-wardens continues 'till new Church-wardens are sworn; and if they refuse to take the Oath as the Law directs, being duly elected, they may be excommunicated. Before the Church-wardens are sworn, they can do no legal Act as Church-wardens, nor have they any Authority, but whatever they do is of their own Wrong. *Con.89.*

Besides the Care of the Repairs of the Church, Seats, *etc.* which I shall mention hereafter; Church-wardens are to see that the Parishioners come to Church every *Sunday*, and to present the Names of such who absent, to the Ordinary; or levy 1s. for every Offence. *Stat. 1 Eliz. c.1.*

They are not to permit any to stand idle, walk or talk in the Church or Church-yard; to take Care that no Persons sit in the Church with their Hats on, or in any other indecent Manner; but that they behave themselves orderly, soberly and reverently, kneeling at the Prayers, and standing at the Belief, *etc.* that none contend about Places, and they may chastise disorderly Boys, *etc. Can.18,* and *111.*

The Church-wardens shall suffer no Man to preach within their Churches or Chapels, without producing their Licence; and take Care that all Persons excommunicated be kept out of the Church. *Can.50, 85.* and to see that Peace be duly kept in the Congregation.

All quarrelling is prohibited either in the Church or Church-yard; and if any offend in such Case, the Ordinary may suspend him from entring the Church, *etc.* Where one is assaulted and beaten in a Church, it is not lawful to return Blows in his own Defence; for striking or laying Hands on another there, the Offender shall be excommunicated. *5 & 6 Ed.6. c.4.; 2 Cro.462*

They are to apprehend those who interrupt, or disturb the Minister, and bring them before a Justice of Peace, *etc.* and disturbing the Minister, by Statute *2 & 3 Ed.6.* is liable to a Penalty of £10 and three Months Imprisonment; for the second Offence to forfeit £20 or suffer six Months Imprisonment; and for the third Offence, shall forfeit all Goods and Chattels, and be imprison'd during Life. By *1 Eliz. c.1.* to forfeit an hundred Marks, *etc.* And by *1 W. & M.* to disturb a Congregation, misuse a Teacher, *etc.* incurs a Forfeiture of £20.

Church-wardens, *etc.* shall see that the Lord's Day be duly observed; search Ale-houses on *Sundays*, and if they find any Persons therein, during Divine Service, they are to make them pay 3s. 4d. and also 1s. for being absent from Church; and the Master of the House shall forfeit 10s. *etc. Stat. 1 Jac.1. cap.9.*

They are to execute Warrants against such who profane the Lord's Day; and levy the Forfeiture of 1s. *etc.* on those who curse or swear, by Warrant from a Justice, *etc.*

Persons doing any worldly Labour on a *Sunday*, forfeit 5s. Butchers killing or selling Meat, Carriers travelling, *etc.* **See Constables**.

Church-wardens are to keep the Keys of the Bellfry, and take Care that the Bells be not rung without good Cause, to be allowed of by the Minister and themselves. *Can.88.*

And they are to make Presentment upon Oath, (usually twice a Year) especially at the Visitation of the Bishop, of the several Articles following, *viz.* Whether there be a Box for Alms in the Church; the Bells and Bell-Ropes are in Repair; there be a Bible, Common Prayer Book, and Book of Canons; a Desk for the Reader, Cushion for the Pulpit and a Surplice; a Communion-Table, Table-Cloth, Cups and Covers for Bread, Flaggons and Font; a Carpet, a Register-Book and Chest with three Locks; King's Arms set up, Grave-Stones and Monuments well kept; Lord's Prayer, Creed and Commandments in fair Letters; the Church-yard well fenced, Church and Chancel and Parsonage-House in Repair, *etc.*

Whether the Parson reads the Thirty-nine Articles twice a Year, and the Canons once a Year, preaches every *Sunday* good Doctrine, reads the Common Prayer, celebrates the Sacrament, reads the Homilies, observes the 30th of *January*, the 29th of *May*, and the 5th of *November*, preach in his Gown, wear a Surplice, visit the Sick, bury the Dead, catechise Children, baptise with Godfathers, marry according to Law, live a sober Life.

N. B. Parsons resident on Livings not reading the Common Prayer once a Month, forfeit £5. *13 & 14 Car.2.* And marrying Persons without publishing the Banns or Licence, they shall forfeit £100 the Persons married £10. And Clerks assisting £5. *Stat. 7 & 8 W.3.* In every Parish there shall be a Parish Register, of Christnings, Marriages and Burials, subscribed by the Minister and Church-wardens; and the Names of the Persons are to be transmitted yearly to the Bishop, *etc.*

If any of the Parishioners are Adulterers, Fornicators, Drunkards, Swearers, Blasphemers, resort to Alehouses, *etc.* in Time of Divine Service, work on *Sundays*, not repair to Church, Alms-Houses or Schools abused, Legacies given to pious Uses, Baptism neglected, Women not coming to be churched, marrying in prohibited Degrees, (of which there is to be a Table,) marrying without Banns,

Licence, or at unlawful Hours, if Sacraments received three Times a Year of all above sixteen; Seats, if Parishioners are placed in them without Contention, *etc.* and if they refuse to make Presentment, the Parson and Vicar may present.

By the 117th Canon, Church-wardens are to make their Presentments of such Things which are given in Charge at the Visitation; but not oftner than once a Year, where it hath been no oftner used; nor above twice in any Diocese whatsoever, except it be at the Bishop's Visitation: The general Time of making Presentments is at *Easter.*

And as at the Common Law, Inquiry is to be made of Offences by Juries; so by the Ecclesiastical Laws, Inquest shall be made by Church-wardens, *etc.* But the Presentment which they make must not be with a malicious Design to vex the People; for if so, Action on the Case lies against them. *Cro. Car.285.*

The Church-wardens, with Consent of the Minister, have the Placing the Parishioners in the Seats of the Body of the Church, appointing Pew keepers, *etc.* reserving to the Ordinary a Power to correct the same: and in *London* the Church-wardens have this Authority in themselves by Custom.

Church-wardens are to repair the Seats in the Church, and dispose thereof; but this is in Subordination to the Bishop of the Diocese, who ought of common Right to place or displace such as shall sit therein, unless Custom or Prescription interposeth; there his Jurisdiction ceaseth, and the Temporal Courts give Remedy in Case of Disturbance, *etc. 12 Co.105.; 3 Inst.202.*

But Church-wardens may not prescribe for a Right, (though they have generally the Disposition of the Seats, appointing Gallery-Keepers, *etc.* except in Cathedrals) for the Ordinary's Desisting from acting; they being only a Corporation capable of Goods, and not of Inheritance. *Roll. Abr.*

If there be a Custom in a Parish, that the Church-wardens are to repair the old Seats and erect new ones, and to appoint who shall sit in them; and they do erect a new Seat in the Body of the Church, and appoint a certain Person to sit there; and after the Ordinary decree that another shall have the Seat: In this Case a Prohibition lies against him, for the Custom hath fixed the Power of Disposing the Seats in the Church-wardens. *Roll. Abr.288.*

The Grant of a Seat to one and his Heirs is not good. The Church-wardens of *D.* by Virtue of their Custom disposed of a good Seat to one; and the Ordinary granted the same Seat to another and his Heirs; whereupon a Prohibition was granted. *Winch. Rep.*

The Parson impropriate has a Right to the chief Seat in the Chancel, because he ought to repair it; but by Prescription, another Parishioner may have it. *Noy's Report, Gilson* versus *Right & al'.*

By the Common Law, the Church and Church-yard are the Freehold of the Parson; but the Use of the Body of the Church, and the Repairs thereof, common to all the Parishioners.

A Man may have a Seat in a Church appendant to his House or Estate, and prescribe that he and his Ancestors, or those whose Estate he hath, usually sat there and repaired the Seat; but one cannot prescribe to a Seat in the Body of the Church generally, without shewing that he, and all those he claims from, have Time out of

Mind repaired it. *Roll. Abr. par. 2. 288.*

The Case is the same in an Isle of a Church: For a Prescription for a Man to sit there with his Family, and repair it, makes the Isle peculiar to his House, and he cannot be displaced by any Body. *Cro.367.* And the Ordinary, *etc.* hath no Power over Seats in private Chapels, belonging to particular Families. *Roll. Abr.*

But if a Man erect a Pew in a Church; or hang up a Bell in a Steeple, they thereby become Church Goods, (tho' they are not expressly given to the Church) and he may not afterwards remove them; if he does, the Church-wardens may sue him. *Stat. 10 H.4.*

Church-wardens are to see that the Body of the Church and Steeple are in Repair; but the Chancel is to be repaired by the Parson: And the Church-wardens are not bound to repair any Part of the Church or Isle which any Man claims by Prescription to him or his House. Anciently both the Church and Church-yard were repaired out of the Revenues of the Church, and a fourth Part of them was appropriated for that Purpose.

The Gates, Stiles and Doors leading into the Church-yard, and the Ways therein, are to be kept in due Repair by Church-wardens: But if any one hath a private Door to the Church, or a Way thro' the Church-yard, (which may not be made without the Consent of the Minister, and a Faculty from the Bishop) they must be repaired by him who hath the Use of them. Inhabitants may prescribe to have a Way through a Church-yard, in respect of a Messuage or Land adjoining; they and their Ancestors having always had and repaired the same. *2 Roll. Abr.265.*

Church Reparations extend particularly to Church-yard Walls, the Walls of the Church and Steeple, the Floor, the Pulpit, and the Pews, Windows, Iron-Bars and Glass; the Roof of Timber, with Laths, Nails, *etc.* the Covering of Lead, Tiles, *etc.* the Doors with Locks and Keys; Stairs, Bells, Wheels and Ropes in the Steeple. *Can.85.*

And Parishioners are Chargeable for the Repairs of Ornaments of the Church: The Communion-Table and Coverings, the Communion-Cups, Bible and other Books appointed to be kept in Churches, the Surplice, Pulpit-Cloth and Cushion are accounted Church-Ornaments.

The Expence of all these, the Sexton's Wages, washing the Communion-Cloaths, Candles and Money disbursed by the Church-wardens, are to be raised by a Rate or Tax.

These Rates are to be made by the Church-wardens, and the greater Part of the Parishioners present, after a general Notice given. *1 Vent.367.*

And some of our Law Books tell us, that if the Parishioners (upon publick Notice given them) do not assemble, the Church-wardens and Overseers of the Poor, or the greater Part of them, may make a Rate, and levy it upon the Inhabitants; it being first confirmed by the Ordinary or Archdeacon. *2 Inst.489.*

The Charge is in Respect of the Lands; and therefore if the Owner lives in another Parish, he shall be rated to repair in the Parish where the Lands lie, unless he let the same by Lease; and then he shall be charged in Respect of the Rent reserved; and in such Case, if the Lessee or Farmer is sued for Repairs, he may plead it, and the Court will order the Tax to be divided between the Landlord and him, *viz.* That the Tenant shall contribute in Proportion to the Rent reserved, and the Landlord for so much as the Land is worth above the Rent. *2 Roll. Rep.270.*

As to this being a real Charge upon all the Lands in the Parish, or only upon the Persons in respect of their Lands; the better Opinion is, that 'tis a personal Charge by Reason of the Lands: For where the Owner or Occupier refuses to contribute, the Lands cannot be sequestred, but the Persons may be excommunicated by the Ordinary. A Man shall be charged for the Repairs of the Church where his Lands are; because to this Purpose he is a Parishioner there, tho' he live in another Parish. *Cro. Eliz. 659.; 2 Roll. Abr.289.; 2 Mod.255.*

The Reparations are to be done by the Church-wardens, at the Charge of all the Parishioners of Ability; and the Ecclesiastical Judge may excommunicate them, for any Neglect in not repairing: The Spiritual Court hath original Jurisdiction of Repairs of Churches, and of Rates for the same; and when a Suit is brought in that Court against a Person for his proportionable Part of such Rate, he may be compelled to put in his Answer upon Oath, whether he hath paid or not. *1 Mod.194.; 1 Vent.339.*

If a Church is so much out of Repair, that 'tis necessary to pull it down, in such Case upon a general Warning to the Parishioners, having first obtained the Consent of the Ordinary, the major Part meeting may make a Rate for pulling down the Church, and rebuilding it on the old Foundation, making Vaults, *etc.* and it shall be good: Also it hath been held, that if a Parish be encreas'd, the greater Part of the Parishioners, with Consent of the Bishop, have Power to raise a Tax for the necessary enlarging of the Church. *2 Mod.222.; 1 Mod.237.; 1 Salk.165.*

The Majority of Parishioners may make a Rate for altering the Place of the Communion-Table, and carrying it into the Chancel; or for raising Steps to go up to it, and oblige the whole Parish, for they are compellable to put Things in decent Order, and they can best judge of the Rules of Decency: But the Majority cannot make a Rate to bind the rest for repairing or adorning the Chancel; because that is the Parson's Freehold. If the Church-wardens would set up a new Seat, make a new Gallery, *etc.* where there was none before, they must have the Consent of the major Part of the Parish, and Licence of the Ordinary. And though Church-wardens may repair the Church, *etc.* without consulting the Vestry; in chargeable Repairs, it is Safe to have the Advice of their Neighbours, who are to bear the Charges of them. *5 Co.66.; 57 Poph.137.; 1 Mod.236.*

A Person living in one Parish, and occupying Lands in another, shall not be charged for Ornaments only of the Church where the Lands lie; because the Inhabitants are to be charged for Ornaments in Respect of their personal Estates. *2 Roll. Abr.291.*

For Church Ornaments, the Charge is upon the Personal Estate of the Parishioners, and not upon their Lands; so that if a Rate is made to charge the Land, a Prohibition will be granted: But by Custom, Lands, *etc.* may be liable to it. *2 Roll. Rep.292.; Cro. Eliz.843.; 2 Lutw.1019.*

A Rate or Tax for the Repairs of a Church.

We whose Names are subscribed, do hereby rate and tax all and every the Inhabitants of the Parish of, *etc.* here under mentioned, for and towards the Repairs of the Church of the said Parish, in the several Sums following, *viz.*

	£	s	d
A.B. For one Tenement, *etc.*	0	7	6
C.D. For his Lands called, *etc.*	0	5	0
E.F. For one Messuage,	0	4	0
G.H. For one Tenement called, *etc.*	0	3	0

J.K. & L.M.   Church-wardens   *N.O.* & P.Q.   Overseers of the Poor
J.L. & A.M. Parishioners *etc.*

A Warrant to distrain for a Church-Tax.
To the Church-wardens of the Parish of, etc.

Midd. ss. Whereas Complaint hath been made unto us, by *J.K.* and *L.M.* of, *etc.* Church-wardens of the said Parish, that *C.D. E.F. etc.* have refused or neglected to pay the Sums of Money by legal Assessment rated on them, for and towards the Reparation of the Parish-Church of, *etc.* aforesaid, *viz.* the said *C.D.* the Sum of, *etc.* and the said *E.F. etc.* These are therefore in his Majesty's Name to command you, that you, or any of you, do levy the said several and respective Sums of, *etc.* by Distress and Sale of the Goods of the said *C.D.* and *E.F.* respectively, rendring to them the Overplus, if any be, after the said several Sums and the Charges of the Distress deducted; and in Case there be no Goods, whereof a sufficient Distress may be taken, that then you do certify the same to us, that such further Proceedings may be had as to Justice appertains. *Given, etc.*

Houses, as well as Lands, are chargeable to these Rates. And if a Parish is unequally rated, those who are grieved must plead it in the Spiritual Court, being sued there; but they cannot have a Prohibition. *2 Roll. Abr.291.*

A Man living in one Parish, and holding Land in another, may be taxed towards the new Casting of the Bells of the Parish where his Lands are; for as they are necessary to the People, they are more than Ornaments.

A Man had a Lease of a Stall in a Market-Town, where he sold Goods once a Week, but lived in another Parish; adjudged not chargeable in the Market-Town. *2 Roll.288.*

Persons of a Chapelry, having always christened and buried within themselves, may prescribe to be exempt from repairing the Mother-Church: But if there be a Chapel of Ease where they hear Divine Service, and they bury at another Church, they must contribute to the Repairs of that Church, notwithstanding they repair the Chapel.

No Church new built is esteemed as such in Law 'till Consecration; which being done, the Parishioners are then to repair it: But neither the Ordinary nor Church-wardens can give Leave to bury there, but the Parson only; the Freehold of the Soil being in him. *1 Cro.367.*

If a Question should arise, whether 'tis a Church or Chapel belonging to the Mother-Church, and any Proof can be made that Sacraments have been administred, and the Dead buried, then 'tis by the Law accounted a distinct Church.

Tho' the Freehold of the Church and Church-yard be in the Parson; yet as he can hinder no Parishioner from having a Place in the Body of the Church, so he may not hinder any such from being buried in the Church-yard; but for burying in the Church, it is otherwise. *2 Cro.366.*

The Fee for Breaking the Soil on Burials, belongs to them upon whom the Burden is of Repairing the Pavement; that is to the Parson for the Chancel, and to the Church-wardens for the Body of a Church. *3 Keb.504.; 1 Vent.274.*

A Man may be indicted at Sessions for digging up the Graves of Persons buried, and taking away their Burial Dresses, *etc.* afterwards interring their Bodies again: And by *Co. Lit.113,* it was resolved in this Case, that the Property of the Winding-Sheets remained in the Person who was the Owner when used; and an Offender was found guilty of Felony, but had his Clergy. *Hain's* Case.

If any Person shall draw a Weapon in the Church with an Intent to Strike, or a Stroke shall be given, the Party may be indicted, and have Judgment to lose one of his Ears. *Stat. 5 & 6 Ed.6. cap.4.*

And if any Person shall arrest a Minister or a Lay-Man going to or returning from Church on a *Sunday,* he may be punished by Indictment.

But to return to Church-wardens: They may maintain an Action for defacing a Monument in the Church. *Godb.279.* And so may an Heir by Descent, have an Action against any one who beats down or defaces Coats of Arms, *etc.* of his Ancestor in the Church, or Church-yard. *2 Cro.367.*

If the Organs be taken out of a Church, the Church-wardens may bring an Action of Trespass, tho' the Vicar took them; because they belong to the Parishioners, and not to the Parson: Adjudged *Trin. 12 Jac.1.*

But if any Thing belonging to the Freehold be broken or cut down, the Walls, Windows, Doors or Trees in the Church-yard, *etc.* the Parson or Vicar, and not the Church-wardens, shall have an Action. *Stat. 8 H.6.* The Soil and Feed of the Church-yard are the Minister's, and the Trees growing therein; but he is not to cut them down, unless for Repairs of the Chancel, *etc.* tho' he may top them. *35 Edw.1.*

Church-wardens are a Corporation only as to moveable Goods, for the Use of the Church, and they may purchase such Goods and Chattels; and also sue or be sued for or concerning such Goods, but for the Use of the Parish. *1 Roll. Abr.393.*

For they cannot prescribe by the Name of Church-wardens to have Lands, *etc.* (except it be in *London:*) Neither can they have any Action at Common Law to recover Goods, Money given, *etc.* of which they were never possessed: But if they had Possession, then they may bring an Action and recover Damages to the Use of the Parish, if such Goods are taken away and abused: And they may recover Goods by Bill in Equity which they never had Possession of; but they cannot sell or dispose of them without the Assent of the Parish; if they do, the Parishioners may chuse new Officers, who may bring Action of Account against them. *Coke's Rep.3 par. Hadman's* Case.

The Compleat Parish Officer - Church-wardens.

In the City of *London*, by special Custom, the Church-wardens with the Minister make a Corporation for Lands as well as for Goods; and may as such, hold, purchase and take Lands for the Use of the Church, and sue and be sued on the Account thereof. And there is another Custom in *London*, for the Parishioners to chuse both Church-wardens, exclusive of the Minister; who is also there excused from repairing the Chancel of the Church. *2 Cro.325.; 1 Co. Inst.3.; 1 Roll. Abr.339.*

Church-wardens of every Parish within the Weekly Bills of Mortality, shall, at the Charge of their respective Parishes, fix upon the Pipes belonging to the Water-works, Stop-blocks and *Fire Cocks*; and make a Mark on the Front of any House over against them to find them, where an Instrument is to be kept to open the Plug when any Fire happens. *Stat. 6 Ann. c.31.*

And in each Parish is to be kept a large Engine, and a Hand-Engine, and a Leather Pipe and Socket of the same Size as the Plug or Fire-Cock, under the Penalty of £10 to be levied by Warrant of two Justices by Distress and Sale of the Goods of the Church-wardens; one Moiety to go to the Informer, and the other to the Poor. *Stat. Ibid.*

The first Person who brings in a Parish-Engine, or any other large Engine with a Socket, *etc.* when any Fire happens, shall be paid as an Encouragement 30s. the Person who brings in the second Parish-Engine, shall be paid 20s. the third 10s. and the Turn-Cock, whose Water shall first come into the main Pipe, is to have 10s. paid by the Church-wardens; or the same shall be levied by Distress, *etc. Stat. 7 Ann. c.17.*

And the Church-wardens and Overseers of Poor may make Rates and Assessments for Money for the Maintenance and Repairs of Engines, Stop-blocks, *etc.* as they do for the Maintenance of the Poor, *etc. Stat. Ibid.*

Church-wardens are to account at the End of the Year, and deliver what remains in their Hands to their Successors, by Writing indented; and if they refuse, they may be presented at the next Visitation, or the new Church-wardens may have an Action against them at Common Law: But they shall be allowed all necessary Disbursements. And if they have not gather'd their Rates, they are to prosecute Persons before they leave their Office; present them in their last Presentment, or pass over their Arrears to their Successors, who shall recover the same for them. *Can.88, 89, 109.; 1 Roll. Abr.121.*

When Church-wardens Receipts fall short of their Disbursements, the succeeding Church-wardens ought to pay them the Ballance, and place it to their Account, by the *Canon 88*. At the same Time that the Church-wardens pass their Accounts of all Money receiv'd and expended during their Office; they must also give an Account of the Church Goods committed to their Charge, which shall be then brought forth, call'd over and examin'd, and after that deliver'd over to the Successors, together with the Keys of the Parish Chest, *etc.*

If any Dispute arise about the Account, it is to be decided before the Ordinary: And for Disbursement of any Sum not exceeding 40s. the Church-warden's Oath alone is a sufficient Proof; but for all Sums above 40s. Receipts must be produced, *etc.* No Allowance of Account can discharge Church-wardens of any fraudulent

Dealings, which they may have been Guilty of in their Office; but whenever any such are detected, they are accountable, and every Parishioner hath a Right to claim Justice against them. And though all the Parish have allow'd Accounts of the Church Goods, the Ordinary may call them to account before him too, and punish them if he find Cause; but in laying out Money, they are punishable for Fraud only, not Indiscretion. *2 Roll. Abr.120.*

Church-wardens have the Care of the Benefice during its Vacancy; and as soon as there shall be any Avoidance, they are to apply to the Chancellor of the Diocese for a Sequestration; and having taken out an Instrument for it, they are to manage all the Profits and Expences of the Benefice for him that shall next succeed: Plow and sow his Glebes, take in the Crop, gather in Tithes, thresh out and sell Corn, repair Houses, Fences, *etc.* but not commit Waste upon the Living, in cutting Timber, *etc.* And they are to take Care, that during the Vacancy, the Church be duly serv'd by a Curate approv'd by the Bishop, whom they are to pay out of the Profits of the Benefice. *2 Co. Inst.89.*

If Church-wardens through Improvidence, Indiscretion or Negligence, waste the Church Goods in their Custody, or much damnify the Parish, on Proof thereof, they may be remov'd at any Time, by the Authority of the Ordinary. *8 El. 4, 6.; 13 Co.70.*

They are to join with Constables in making Rates for Relief of poor Prisoners, maimed Soldiers, *etc.* and in chusing Surveyors of the Highways, appointing Days to work, *etc.* and they must join with Overseers of the Poor in the Execution of their whole Office.

Of Sidesmen (Synodsmen) or Questmen.

Sidesmen are those Officers that are yearly chosen in great Parishes, in *London* and other Cities, to assist the Church-wardens in making Inquests and Presentments of such Offences and Offenders to the Ordinary in his Episcopal *Synod*, as are punishable in the Spiritual Court.

These Sidesmen shall be chosen in *Easter* Week, by the Minister and Parishioners; or if they cannot agree, to be appointed by the Ordinary; and take an *Oath* that they will assist the Church-wardens in the Execution of their Office, so far as by Law they are bound.

They are diligently to see that all the Parishioners duly resort to the Church upon all *Sundays* and *Holidays*, and there continue during the whole Time of Divine Service, *etc.* And all such as shall be found negligent in resorting to the Church, they shall call upon, and after due Admonition, present them to the Ordinary of the Place. *Can.90.*

No Church-wardens, Sidesmen or Questmen, shall be cited or call'd but only at the Times limited and appointed to appear in the Ecclesiastical Court, for refusing to present any Faults or Offences committed in their Parishes at other Times; nor be further troubled after their Presentments deliver'd at the usual Time, unless it appear that they have wilfully omitted for Favour, *etc.* to present some notorious publick Crime or Crimes; or upon just Cause to call them in order to explain their former Presentments, *etc.* But in Case of any wilful Omission of their Duty, the Ordinary may proceed against them for Breach of Oath, as in Cases for wilful

Perjury. *Can. 117.*

A Warrant against Sabbath-breakers.

To the Constables, Church-wardens, Sidesmen, and Overseers of the Poor of the Parish of, etc.

Midd. ss. Whereas we *A.B.* and *C.D.* Esqrs; two of his Majesty's Justices of Peace for, *etc.* have been informed, that the Lord's Day is often prophaned in your Parish, by disorderly Meetings of several idle Persons, and by Gaming, Sports, and Tipling in publick Houses and Shops, and by Persons using their Trades and Callings on that Day, contrary to the Laws in that Case made and provided; which disorderly and unlawful Proceedings, tend to the Encouragement of Vice, Lewdness and Immorality, to the great Dishonour of GOD, Disturbance of the Inhabitants, and evil Example to others: These are therefore in his Majesty's Name to require you, and every of you, to make strict and diligent Search throughout your said Parish, on the next Lord's Day, being the, *etc.* for all such Persons offending as aforesaid; and that you take a true Account of all and every the Persons offending in the Premises, to the End the same may be return'd by you upon Oath unto us at Petty Sessions to be held at, *etc.* on, *etc.* in order to inflict such Penalties upon them as the Law in that Case requires; and herein you are not to fail. *Given under our Hands, etc.*

Of Briefs, and their Management.

The Statute *4 & 5 Ann. c. 14.* enacts, That when Copies of Briefs are deliver'd to the Wardens of Churches and Chapels, *etc.* immediately after Receipt, they are to indorse the Time of Receiving, with their Names thereon; and forthwith deliver them over to the Ministers and Curates, who shall likewise indorse the Time of their Receipt, and their Names, in like Manner as the Church-wardens.

The Ministers, Curates and Preachers, on some *Sunday*, in two Months after Receipt thereof, are immediately before Preaching openly to read such Briefs in their respective Places of Meeting; and the Church-wardens shall collect the Money that shall be given there, or go from House to House, *etc.*

The Sums collected, Place and Time, are to be indorsed in Words at Length, and signed by the Minister, Curate and Church-wardens, and by the Teacher and two substantial Persons of separate Congregations: And the Briefs indorsed, and Money collected shall be delivered to the Persons undertaking the Brief, under the Penalty of £20. The Undertakers not demanding the Briefs and Money in six Months, are liable to the same Penalty.

If the whole Number of Briefs be not return'd, the Undertaker for every Copy wanting, shall forfeit £50 unless he make sufficient Proof in Chancery of the Briefs being lost by inevitable Accident, and of the Money collected thereupon. And a Register is to be kept of all Monies collected, inserting the Occasion of the Brief, and the Time when collected; to which all Persons may have a free Resort.

The Undertakers in two Months after the Receipts of the Money, and Notice to Sufferers, are to account before a Master in Chancery, to be appointed before the Lord Chancellor.

All Farming and Purchasing such Charity-Money, is declared unlawful; and Deeds of Covenant and Agreement concerning the same shall be void: And any Person agreeing to purchase the Benefit of such Brief, shall forfeit £500 for the

Benefit of the Sufferers.

Of Parochial Libraries.

By a Statute made *7 Ann. c.4.* it is enacted that Libraries, erected in Parishes, shall be preserv'd for the Uses directed by the Founders.

And where a Parochial Library is appropriated to the Use of the Incumbent, he must within six Months after his Induction, make a Catalogue of all Books in the Library, and sign the same, acknowledging the Possession of such Books, which Catalogue is to be deliver'd to the Ordinary.

And upon the Death of an Incumbent, the Library shall be lock'd up by the Church-wardens, or a Person appointed by the proper Ordinary. None of the Books shall be alienable, without the Consent of the Ordinary, and then only when there is a Duplicate of such Books. And if any Book shall be taken away or detain'd, a Justice of Peace may grant his Warrant to search for the same, and order it to be restor'd.

Also Action of Trover may be brought in the Name of the Ordinary, in which treble Damages and full Costs shall be recover'd.

Act for building fifty new Churches in London *and* Westminster.

1. By the Statute *9 Ann. c.22.* A Duty of 2s. *per* Chalder is laid upon all Coals imported in *London*, for a certain Term or Number of Years.

2. The Money arising by this Duty is to be paid into the Exchequer, and appropriated for building fifty new Churches of Stone with Towers or Steeples, and for purchasing Sites of Churches, Church-yards, *etc.* in or near *London* and *Westminster*, and for making Chapels already built Parish-Churches, such as are capable thereof, *etc.*

3. The Queen, by Letters Patent, may nominate Commissioners, who shall meet as often as there is Occasion, and inform themselves in what Parishes the new Churches are most necessary to be built, and of proper Places to build them in, and of Church-yards and burying Places to be bought; and no Burials are to be in or under any of the new Churches.

4. The Commissioners, or any five of them, may agree and Contract for the Purchase of Lands for the said new Churches, for Church-yards, and for Ministers Houses: The Lands purchased shall be conveyed to the Commissioners and their Heirs; and they are to cause the Churches to be built, provide Houses for Ministers, Church-yards to be inclosed, *etc.*

5. They may by Parchment-writing under their Hands and Seals enrolled in Chancery, ascertain the Bounds to each new Church and Church-yard; and also the District of each Parish that shall be appointed for every new Church: And after the Inrollment of such Writing and Consecration of the Church, such District shall be taken to be a distinct Parish; and the Inhabitants within that District shall be Parishioners thereof, and subject to all Taxes, Rates for the Poor, *etc.* as the Inhabitants in the Parish from whence such new Parish was taken, are chargeable; but shall be exempted from bearing any Office or Charge in the other Parish.

6. There shall be a Rector in every new Church; and a Morning Preacher in a Chapel converted into a Parish Church, who has officiated therein for a Month before the Consecration, who shall be the first Rector of the new Church; and in

every other new Church the first Rector is to be appointed by the Queen; and he and his Successors shall be called the Rector of such new Church; and the Freehold shall be in him and his Successors, and he and they may purchase and take Lands to the Value of £200 *per Ann.*

7. Any Person whatsoever may contract and agree with five or more of the Commissioners for any Lands, *etc.* or for limiting or settling the Right of Patronage, and Presentation of the succeeding Rectors; and until such Settlement can be made of the Right of Patronage in every new Parish, the Crown shall present on any Avoidance.

8. The Rectors of the new Churches, and the Church-wardens, shall be subject to the Ordinary; and the Bishop of *London* is to visit, institute and exercise Ecclesiastical Jurisdiction in all Parishes, to be erected, *etc.*

9. The first Church-wardens, Overseers of the Poor, Surveyors of the Highways, and other Parish-Officers, of every new Parish are to be elected by five or more of the Commissioners out of the Inhabitants, within a Month after the Consecration of each Church: And the said Parish Officers shall have the like Powers, and be subject to the same Laws as any other in *London* and *Westminster*, and all the succeeding Parish-Officers shall be chosen and sworn yearly in every new Parish, according to the Laws now in Force.

10. Five or more of the Commissioners, with the Consent of the Ordinary, may name a sufficient Number of the Inhabitants of each new Parish to be Vestrymen; and upon the Death or Removal, *etc.* of any Vestryman, the rest, or the Majority, may chuse another, being an Inhabitant and Housholder in the Parish. But all parochial Customs, By-Laws, *etc.* used in any Parish divided, shall, notwithstanding such Division, continue in both Parishes.

11. Five or more of the Commissioners, with the Consent of the present Rectors, Church-wardens, Vestry, *etc.* Or the Rectors, Vicars, Parish-Officers, and Vestrymen or principal Inhabitants, with the Consent of the Ordinary, by Writing inrolled in Chancery, may make a perpetual Division of Parishes, as to Church Rates, Rates for the Poor, Highways, *etc.* and until such Division be made, the Parish Rates, shall be assessed and levied through all Parts which now belong to the present Parishes.

12. The Parish-Officers, with the Vestry or principal Inhabitants of the new Parishes, are to meet every Year, on *Tuesday* in *Easter*-Week, or oftner, on Notice given the *Sunday* before in the Church; and there assess the Rates for the Poor, and other Parish-Rates, and apportion the said Rates, to be collected for the Relief of the Poor.

By *Stat. 1 Geo.1. c.23.* A Duty is granted on Coals imported in *London*, to be appropriated for the Maintenance of Ministers for the Fifty new Churches; and the King to appoint Commissioners to execute Powers, *etc.*

The *12 Geo.1. c.39* makes a particular Provision for the Rector of *St. Mary le Strand*, and ordains that the said Rector shall have the Interest of the Sum of £2,500 out of the Money directed by the Act *1 Geo.1.* And for a further Maintenance £125 *per Ann.* to be raised by an equal Pound-Rate on the Inhabitants within the District appointed for the said Parish; and the Rector, Church-wardens and Vestry are impowered to make Assessments, being allowed by two Justices of Peace, *etc.* also the Sum assessed shall be yearly collected by such Persons as the Vestry or Church-wardens shall nominate, for whom the Parish is to be answerable, *etc.*

And the *Stat. 1 Geo.2. c.19.* Enacts, that for raising a Maintenance for the Rector of the new Parish near *Milbank* in the Parish of St. *Margaret Westminster*, £2,500 shall be allotted for his Share of £360,000 appropriated for the Churches, to be laid out in the Purchase of Lands, *etc.* for the Use of the said Rector, by Order of the Commissioners, *etc.* And also the Sum of £125 a Year shall be raised on the Inhabitants, by an equal Pound-Rate, made by the Rector, Church-wardens, *etc.* over and above Fees and Perquisites; payable quarterly, in Lieu of Tithes, *etc.* subject to some Deductions to the present Curate.

By the *2 Geo.2. c.10.* a Maintenance is provided for the Minister of the new Parish or Hamblet of *Spittle Fields, viz.* £3,000 and £125 *per Ann.* to be paid by the Church-wardens, out of Money raised for Burials, Vaults, Monuments, *etc.*

And by *2 Geo.1. c.30.* The like Provision is made for the Minister of the new Church of *Wapping Stepney.*

The *3 Geo.2. c.3.* provides for the Minister of the Parish of St. *Mary Stratford Bow*, in the County of *Middlesex, viz.* £3,500 to be laid out in the Purchase of Lands, *etc.* and £40 a Year to be raised by the Church-wardens, on Pews, *etc.* for the Use of the Rector.

By *Stat. 3 Geo.2. c.17.* A Provision or Maintenance of £3,500 and £60 *per Ann.* is made and appointed for the Minister of the new Church at *Lime house.*

And by *3 Geo.2. c.23.* The Sum of £3,500 and £70 a Year payable by Church-wardens, *etc.* is ordered for the Minister of the new Parish-Church of St. *Nicholas Deptford*, in the Counties of *Kent* and *Surrey.*

The *Stat. 6 Geo.2. c.8.* was made for rebuilding the Church of St. *George the Martyr*, in the Borough of *Southwark*, as one of the Fifty new Churches, appointing £6,000 for that Purpose, *etc.*

And the *6 Geo.2. c.21.* provides a Maintenance for the Rector of the new Church near *Old-street*, in the Parish of St. *Giles Cripplegate; viz.* £3,500 to be laid out on Lands, and £120 *per Annum, etc.*

Of Vestries and Vestrymen.

A Vestry is the Assembly of the whole Parish, met together for the Dispatch of the Business of the Parish; and this Meeting being commonly held in the Place for keeping the Priest's Vestments, adjoining or belonging to the Church, it thence has its Name of Vestry.

In former Times, the Bishops and beneficed Priests sat together in Vestries, to consult of the Affairs of the Church; in Imitation of which, the Minister, Church-wardens and chief Men of Parishes, do at this Day make a Parish Vestry.

Antiently every Parishioner who paid to the Church-Rates, or Scot and Lot, had a Right to come to these Meetings; and when they who are thus qualified, are assembled at the Time and Place appointed, all that are absent shall be concluded by a Majority of those who are present. But in large populous Parishes, a Custom has obtained of yearly chusing a certain Number of the chiefest and most reputable Men to represent all the Rest, who are called a *Select Vestry*.

But Select Vestries having been thought oppressive and injurious in some Parishes, the Power of them hath been contested: And not long since the Select Vestries of *St. Saviours* and *St. Olave* in *Southwark* were set aside and demolished; but the Select Vestry of *St. Mary Hill* in *London*, and of the Parish of *Massam* in *Yorkshire*, on due Proof of Custom and Usage, were allowed and confirmed in *B.R.; Mich. 2; W. & M. ; 2 Lutw.1027.*

By Custom there may be a Vestry chosen, to have the Government of a Parish, make Rates, and take Accounts of Church-wardens, *etc.* And Vestrymen are a Select Number of the chief Parishioners, in every Parish within the City of *London*, *etc.* who yearly chuse Officers for the Parish, and take Care of its Concernments, by Statute: And these Vestrymen are to make a Declaration or Acknowledgment, that they will conform to the Liturgy of the Church of *England*, as by Law established, *etc. Stat. 15 Car.2. c.2.* and *5.*

In the Election of Vestrymen, those that do not pay to the Church-Rates have no Votes; except the Parson or Vicar. When any Rates are made, the Parishioners must have Notice of a Vestry held for that Purpose; and the Sunday before any Vestry is to meet, this Notice ought to be given, either in the Church after Divine Service, or at the Church Door, both of the Time and Place of the Assembling, and for what Business; and 'tis usual for one of the Church-Bells to be tolled half an Hour before the Vestry begins, and when the Parishioners are met, the major Part present conclude all the others; but to make their Consent more authentick, 'tis necessary that every such Act be entered by the Vestry Clerk in the Parish-Book, and that every Man consenting set his Hand thereto. *5 Rep.66.; Hetley 61.; 1 Mod.194, 236.; 2 Mod.222.*

Action of the Case lies against a Vestry Clerk, for shutting a Parishioner out of the Vestry-room, who hath a Right to be present and vote in the Vestry, at the making of Rates, *etc.* for this Action is his proper and only Remedy; there being no Breach of the Peace, or Damage to the Publick, to have Remedy by Indictment, or Information: This was held by the Court; tho' it was insisted, that the Action would not lie, because it might encourage Multiplicity of Actions against one Person for the same Offence, and the Plaintiff ought to set forth some particular Damage done him.

But the Plaintiff is to shew a legal or prescriptive Right in the Parishioners to meet at a Vestry; and set forth a Right in himself, to enter the Room where the Vestry was kept; for otherwise it may be the Room of the Defendant, where he hath no Right to come. *Pasih. 8 Geo.1.; Phylibrown v. Ryland, Mod.Cas.L. & E. 354.*

The Statute made *9 Ann. c.22.* for Building the Fifty New Churches in *London* and *Westminster*, as I have before observ'd, ordains, that Five or more of the Commissioners shall have Power, with the Consent of the Ordinary, by Writing under their Hands and Seals enrolled in *Chancery*, to name Vestrymen for each new Parish erected; and on the Death of any Vestryman, *etc.* the Rest of them may chuse another, out of the Inhabitants and Housholders of the Parish.

By the Statute *2 Geo.2. c.10.* made for the raising a Maintenance for the Rector of the new Church built in *Spittle-Fields*, 'tis enacted, that the Rector of that Church, and Church-wardens and Overseers of the Poor of that new Parish, and all other Persons who have served or paid Fines for being excused from serving those Offices, shall be the Vestrymen for the Time being, and meet on publick Notice; and the said Vestrymen shall elect and nominate a Lecturer, Church-wardens, Sidesmen, Parish-Clerk, and other Officers of the Church and Parish, *etc.*

By Statute *2 Geo.2. c.30.* for providing for the Rector of *Wapping-Stepney* new Church; the Rector, Church-wardens and Overseers of the Poor for the Time being, and all others who shall pay two Shillings a Month or more, towards the Relief of the Poor, and none other Persons, shall be Vestrymen of that new Parish; and have the same Powers, *etc. ut supra.*

And by the Statute *3 Geo.2. c.33.* for raising a Maintenance for the Minister of the new Parish-Church of *St. Nicholas Deptford*, it is ordained, that the Minister, Church-wardens, Overseers of the Poor, and all other Parishioners, who shall pay to the Relief of the Poor, shall be Vestrymen of that new Parish; and shall meet, and have the same Powers, *etc. supra.*

And the like Clauses are inserted in divers other Statutes, concerning other new Parish-Churches.

The Statute *7 Ann. c.17.* enacts, that the Church-wardens, Overseers and Principal Inhabitants of Parishes in a Vestry, shall rate and assess competent Sums for defraying the Charge of Engines, *etc.* in every Parish within the Bills of Mortality.

And Vestries of Parishes are to be consulted by Church-wardens and Overseers of the Poor, and give their Consent to the Hiring of Houses for the better Employment and Maintenance of the Poor, by *9 Geo.1. c.7.*

Of the Vestry-Clerk, and Beadle.

The Vestry-Clerk is chosen by the Vestry, and acts as their Register or Secretary; and he has the Custody of all Books and Papers relating thereunto.

The *Beadle* of a Parish is also one chosen by the Vestry, whose Business is to attend it; and generally to do and execute all the Orders and Business of the Vestry and Parish, as their Messenger or Servant; he is to assist the Constables in taking up Beggars, passing Vagrants, *etc.* And where they are to be passed to a great Distance, he is sometimes inserted among the Overseers of the Poor, *etc.*

OVERSEERS OF THE POOR, *ETC.*

These Officers were created by the Statute *43 Eliz. c.2.* (the first Statute-Law made for Relief of the Poor) and they are called Overseers, as they have the Government of the Poor.

They are usually nominated in *Easter*-Week, or within a Month after, out of the substantial Housholders, by Appointment under the Hand and Seal of two Justices, residing in or near the Parish or Division where the Parish lieth.

Justices of the Peace neglecting to nominate Overseers of the Poor, and Mayors, and Head Officers of the Town or Place where Default shall happen, forfeit £5 to be employed towards the Relief of the Poor.

The Compleat Parish Officer - Overseers of the Poor.

These Overseers are to meet once a Month in their respective Parish-Churches, to consider of proper Methods for the Relief of and providing for the Poor; and every one absenting himself from such monthly Meeting, not being sick, or having some just Excuse to be allowed by two Justices, is to forfeit 20s. for every Default.

Church-wardens shall likewise meet once a Month with the Overseers of the Poor, or they may be punished for their Neglects; by which it appears that they have an equal Power and Charge with the Overseers.

Overseers are to take Care that the Poor be set at Work, or relieved if not able, and to settle them in their Habitations.

But none are to be relieved, whose Names are not registred in a Parish-Book, kept for that Purpose; unless by Authority under the Hand and Seal of a Justice, (on Oath made of Cause, and Refusal of Relief by Overseers, *etc.* by new Act *9 Geo.1.*) or in Case of pestilential Diseases, *viz.* the Plague, or the Small-Pox, in respect of their Families only. *Stat. 3 & 4 W. & M. c.11.*

Persons relieved must have, on the uppermost Garment, and upon the Shoulder of the right Sleeve, a large Letter P. and the first Letter of the Parish; or otherwise one Justice, upon Complaint, may cause their Allowances to be abridged or suspended, or may commit the Offenders to the House of Correction, not exceeding one and twenty Days. *Stat. 8 & 9 W. c.30.*

Officers relieving those who do not wear the Badge forfeit 20s. for every Offence; one Moiety to the Informer, the other to the Poor.

Overseers may license poor Persons to beg for Alms in their own Parishes; and if any Inhabitants serve Poor at their Doors, not being of their own Parish, and having such a License, they shall forfeit 10s. *Dalt.157.*

There are reckon'd three Sorts of poor People; such as are poor by Impotency, (which takes in the Aged, Decrepit, Lame, Blind, distracted Persons, Infants, *etc.*) such as become Poor by Casualty, (which includes Persons maimed, undone by Fire, overcharged with Children) and such as have made themselves poor by Rioting, Idleness, Drunkenness, *etc.*

As to the first Sort, the Poor by Impotency, the Overseers are to provide for them a necessary Relief and Allowance.

As for the second Sort of Poor, those by Casualty, if they are of Ability and Strength, they are to be set on Work by the Overseers, and to be further relieved according to their Necessities.

But for the third Sort, they are not to be relieved, except it be in Cases of great Extremity; but are to be sent to the House of Correction, and there set at Work to maintain themselves by hard Labour. *Dalt.157, etc.* And in every County, there is to be a House of Correction, or the Justices shall be fined, *etc. 39 Eliz.*

In present Exigencies Overseers are to provide for Poor, and it is discretionary to give them Money, or Victuals, *etc.* And they may be re-imbursed by general Order of Justices in Sessions. *Style 246.; 1 Keb.336.*

Overseers are to set at Work all Persons as have no visible Income to maintain themselves, or follow no Trade or Business to get their Livelihoods; and they may, with the Consent of two Justices of Peace set up any Trade, Mystery or Occupation for the setting on Work and relieving the Poor of the Parish or Place. *Stat. 3 Car.1. c.4.* Children of all such whose Parents shall not, by the Church-wardens and

Overseers, be thought able to keep them, are to be thus set at Work. *43 Eliz. 2*. And any Justice may send to the House of Correction, *etc*. Persons refusing to be employ'd in Work.

The Overseers of the Poor shall within four Days after the End of the Year, and after other Overseers are nominated, give up their Accounts before two Justices, of all Money receiv'd by them, or what is assess'd, and not receiv'd; what Poor they have reliev'd, what Stock they or the Poor have in their Hands, and of all other Things belonging to their Office, and shall pay and deliver over what is in their Hands to the new Church-wardens and Overseers. *Stat. 43 Eliz. c.2.*

And as often as Overseers of the Poor yield up their Accounts to the Justices, they shall give in the Name and Quality of every Person buried within the Parish, from the Time of their former Account; and of such Certificates as came to their Hands from the Parson, *etc*. of Persons interr'd contrary to the Statute *30 Car.2. c.3.* for burying in Woollen; and also of their levying the Penalty of £5 and give an Account of the Disposal of the same, or they shall forfeit £5. And their Accounts shall not be allowed, till they have accounted for the Burials. Affidavit is to be made in eight Days, that a Person was buried in Woollen.

If Overseers refuse to account, or to deliver over what remains in their Hands to their Successors, two Justices may commit them to Gaol, there to remain without Bail, till they account and pay over the Money; or, in the last Case, the same may be levied by Distress. *Stat. 43 Eliz.*

If an Overseer makes a false Account, he may be bound over to the Sessions, and there indicted, *etc. Dalton's* Justice *154.* And in Actions brought against Overseers of the Poor, for misspending the Parish's Money, any Parishioners not receiving Alms, shall be admitted as Evidence. *Stat. 3 & 4 W. & M.*

Overseers are not oblig'd to disburse any of their own Money for the Relief of the Poor; but if they do, a Rate ought to be made to re-imburse them; and the Overseers may make a Rate for that Purpose, and when the Money is levied, pay themselves; and if the Justices refuse to sign it, then a *Mandamus* may be issued, requiring them to do it. *2 Keb.* The King *adversus* Ogden, *Mod. Cases 97.*

But if an Overseer be obstinate, and will not disburse any Thing; the Justices may compel him, and make a Tax for the Poor of themselves. *Per* Windham.

Of the Poors Rate and Taxation.

Overseers of the Poor have Power to Rate and Tax every Inhabitant and Occupier of Houses, Lands, Tithes, Underwoods, Mines, *etc*. to raise Money towards the Relief of the Poor, providing a competent Stock of Flax, Hemp, *etc*. to set the Poor on Work, and also for the putting out Poor Children Apprentices; which Rate being allow'd by two Justices, the Church-wardens and Overseers may levy the same by Distress and Sale, and for Want of Distress, the Party may be committed to Gaol till Payment. *43 Eliz. c.2.*

All Persons, the Clergy not excepted, must contribute to the Relief of the Poor. *2 Keb.251.* And all Things that bring in an annual Profit, may be taxed; Tolls are taxable. *3 Keb. 594.*

But if the Overseers make an unequal Rate, they may be indicted for it, and fined. *1 Keb. 173.*

The Compleat Parish Officer -Overseers of the Poor..

All Assessments ought to be made according to the visible Estate the Party hath or possesseth in the Parish where the Assessment is made, and not elsewhere; the Words of the Act directing a Taxation on the Occupiers. *2 Bulstr.354.*

The Tax is to be in Proportion to the yearly Value, and not the Quantity of Land; and as it arises by Reason of the Land in the Parish, the Farmer or Renter is to pay it, and not the Landlord; and the Landlord is never assess'd for his Rent.

It is either upon Lands or Goods; but a Farmer being assessed for the Land he occupieth, shall not be assessed for his Stock on that Land, necessary for Manure, nor the Profits for which he has been already taxed; but for other Stock he is taxable. And a Clothier, *etc.* having an Estate in Lands, and a great Stock of Wares, may be taxed for both. *Blackerby's Cases 203, etc.*

When Goods are rated, it ought to be after the Value of Lands, (*viz.*) Goods of the Value of £100 should be rated at £5 *per Ann.* or as Lands are; and Persons must be charged only in that Place where the Goods are at the Time of Assessment; as in Case of Lands.

And if a Man hath no Goods where assessed, and is distrained, he may have an Action of Trespass, *etc.*

Overseers of a Parish in Reputation, tho' it be really no Parish, may make Rates for their Poor, and distrain for the Non-payment of them. *Cro. Car.92. Hilton* versus *Pawle.* And the Inhabitants of a Village, having a Chapel and parochial Rights, shall not be taxed to the Poor of the Rectory. *Roll. Rep.160. Contra,* if no parochial Rights.

The Inhabitants of *Lancashire, Cheshire, Yorkshire, Northumberland, Durham, Cumberland,* and *Westmorland,* by Reason of the Largeness of their Parishes, are to have Overseers, and relieve and provide for the Poor within their respective Townships, or Villages, as in Parishes. *Stat. 13 & 14 Car.2.* And other Counties in *England* and *Wales* are mentioned generally in the Preamble of the Act.

If a Parish extends into two Counties or Liberties, the Overseers are to act in the whole Parish, and not divide themselves; but the Justices shall not intermeddle with that Part which lies out of their Jurisdiction. *1 Vent.350.*

But if there be a Church-warden and several Overseers of the Poor, some for Part of the Parish in one County, and others for the other Part in the other County, and the Rates are several, and Accounts separate, they shall be taken as distinct Parishes: The Case of St. *Botelph* without *Aldersgate,* lying Part in *London,* and Part in the County of *Middlesex. Raym.477.*

If a Parish is not able to maintain its own Poor, two Justices may tax any other Parish within the Hundred; and the Sessions have Power to tax the whole County. *Stat. 43 Eliz.* But when the Cause of Taxation of other Parishes, for Inability of those wherein the Poor are resident, ceases, the Tax shall cease also; and the Contribution lessen, as there shall be less Occasion. *Mod.374.; Littleton 73.*

It has been adjudged, that the Justices may tax particular Persons, and need not assess the whole Parish, which is to contribute to the Poor of another Parish. *2 Bulstr.352.*

The Form of an Assessment for the Poor.

A. in Com' Berks, ss. A Rate and Assessment made this Day, *etc.* on the Inhabitants of the Parish of *A.* aforesaid, for and towards the Relief of the Poor there, for the Year, *etc. or,* being the first (or second further Rate) for Relief of the Poor of the said Parish, for the Year 1733 at 9d. in the Pound.

	£	s	d	
A.B. Gent,	0	10	0	
C.D. Yeoman,	0	5	0	
E.F. Merchant,	0	7	6	
G.H. Linen-Draper,	0	6	0	*etc.*

J.K.   Church-warden.   *L.M.* & N.O.   Overseers

We whose Names are under-written, being Inhabitants of the Parish of *A.* aforesaid, have perused the above Rate and Assessment, and do hereby declare, that the several Sums above-mentioned are, by our Approbation, rated upon the respective Persons concerned; and that the same is an equal Rate, according to the best of our Judgments.   *P.Q.*; *R.O.*; J.L.; A.M.   Parishioners   *etc.*

Memorandum, this Day, *etc.* the above Rate and Assessment was ratified and allowed by us, two of his Majesty's Justices of the Peace for the County aforesaid.
                    T.O.   *L.C.*

The Rate being thus confirmed, if any Person shall refuse to pay, *etc.* it may be levied by Warrant from two Justices by Distress; and if that cannot be taken, then two Justices may commit without Bail, 'till Payment (*ut prius.*)

It has been adjudged, that by the Statute, the Poor's Rates ought to be assess'd monthly, and not quarterly, *etc.* for otherwise a Man cannot remove in the Middle of a Quarter, but he will be twice rated; nor can a Distress be taken by a general Warrant made at the Time of the Rate, but there must be a special Warrant; neither can it be taken for a Quarter before it is ended, if the Custom is to rate quarterly. *2 Salk. Rep.532.*

The Quarter-Sessions will relieve such Persons as are grieved by these Rates or Taxes.

The Church-wardens and Overseers of a Parish, made a Rate for the Relief of the Poor, which was confirm'd by two Justices of Peace; but all was rated upon the Real Estates of the Inhabitants, and none on the Personal, and therefore an Appeal was brought to the Quarter-Sessions, where the Rate was quash'd, and the Overseers, *etc.* ordered to make a new Rate upon the Real and Personal Estates. *2 Salk.483.*

In *B.R.* it was objected, that the Sessions had no Power to vacate whole Rates; but adjudged that they may quash such Rates, and refer it to the Church-wardens and Overseers to make new ones, or they may make a new Rate themselves. *Ibid.*

Besides these Rates for Relief of the Poor, there are several Penalties inflicted by Act of Parliament for Offences committed, to be applied to the Use of the Poor;

for which **see under Heads of** *Constables, Church-wardens, Neglects in repairing Highways, Scavengers, etc.*

Relief of poor impotent Persons.

Having treated of Overseers of the Poor in general, I proceed to several Particulars; as the Laws relating to the Relief of impotent Persons, poor Prisoners, *etc.* concerning the placing forth poor Apprentices, Bastardy and Settlements.

A Father, Grandfather, Mother, and Grandmother, and Husband of the Grandmother (being of sufficient Ability) are to maintain and relieve their Children, which are accounted impotent Poor, as the Sessions shall order; under the Penalty of 20s. *per* Month. *43 Eliz. c.2.* But if the Husband of the Grandmother have no Means or Advancement in Marriage with her, he shall not be obliged to keep the Child. *2 Bulstr.345, 347.*

The Husband's having Means, or his being of Ability after Marriage, will not make him liable to the Maintenance of a poor Grandchild, unless the Grandmother had Means sufficient; but if after Marriage, Lands descend to such Grandmother, and the Husband enjoys them in her Right, he shall be bound to keep the Child. A Bastard Child is out of the Statute, and to be provided for otherwise.

A Father has been ordered to allow Maintenance to the Son's Wife, he being beyond Sea; and a Father in Law has been adjudged within the Meaning of the Act. *43 Eliz. Style 283.*

Children of poor, old, impotent Persons, or others, not able to work, are at their own Charges to relieve and maintain them, (in like Manner as Parents are to relieve their Children) if such Children are of Ability, under the like Penalty of 20s. *per* Month, to be levied by Distress and Sale, *etc. per Stat. 43 Eliz. c.2.*

For the better Relief of poor impotent Persons, and to prevent Imposition of Church-wardens and Overseers of the Poor, the Parishioners of every Parish are yearly in *Easter*-Week, or as often as it shall be thought convenient, to meet and examine the Register Book of the Poor; and the Reasons of their taking Relief, *etc.* and to alter the List as they shall see Occasion. *Stat. 3 & 4 W. & M.*

And the Persons receiving Relief are to wear Badges, as has been before observed; (except such Child as shall be permitted to live at Home, to take Care of an impotent and helpless Parent.)

This Statute was made to prevent misapplying Money raised for the impotent and poor, on idle Beggars.

To provide Houses for the Poor, Church-wardens and Overseers, with the Leave of the Lord of the Manor, in Writing under Hand and Seal, or according to any Order set down by Justices of the Peace in their Quarter-Sessions, may build Cottages at the general Charge of the Parish, *etc.* on the Waste, for Habitations of poor impotent Persons; and place Inmates or more Families than one in a Cottage. *Stat. 43 Eliz. c.25.*

The Money for building these Cottages, at the publick Charge of the Parish, may be raised by a Tax, as before directed, *etc.*

A **Petition** *to Justices for an Order for erecting a Cottage.*

To the Worshipful the Justices at the General Quarter-Sessions of the Peace, holden at, *etc.*

The Compleat Parish Officer -Overseers of the Poor..

The Humble Petition of J.D. *of, etc. Sheweth*, That whereas your Petitioner being very poor and impotent, and with his Wife and Children settled as an Inhabitant in the said Parish, *etc.* and at present destitute of an Habitation, hath by Application made to *A.B.* Esq; Lord of the Manor of, *etc.* obtained his Consent, under his Hand and Seal, for your Petitioner to erect and set up a Cottage on the Waste within the Parish of, *etc.* aforesaid, for an Habitation for himself and his Family; if an Order of Sessions can be obtained for Confirmation thereof, as by the Paper hereunto annexed doth appear.

May you therefore be pleased to grant unto your poor Petitioner the Order of this Court, whereby your said Petitioner may set up a Cottage for an Habitation for himself and poor Family, on some convenient Place on the Waste, within the Manor of, *etc.* aforesaid. *And your Petitioner shall ever Pray.*

Where Persons labour under pestilential Diseases, Justices of Peace, Mayors, *etc.* of Cities and Corporations, may set a weekly Tax on the Inhabitants of the Corporation, for Relief of poor Persons infected with the Plague; and if they are not able to pay it, then on Certificate by such Mayors, *etc.* the two next Justices of the County may tax all the Inhabitants within five Miles of the Corporation. *Stat. 1 Jac. c.31.*

Persons refusing to pay the Tax, the same shall be levied by Distress and Sale; and in Default of a Distress, the Party to be committed to Gaol 'till Payment.

The Law is likewise no less careful in providing for poor Prisoners; for the Statute *43 Eliz. c.2.* gives Power to Justices of Peace, at *Easter* Sessions yearly, to rate every Parish at a certain Sum to be paid weekly, no Parish to pay more than 6d. towards Relief of poor Prisoners in the *King's Bench* and *Marshalsea*; and Treasurers for the County are to be chosen at the said *Easter* Sessions, *etc.*

Justices of Peace of every County in their General Quarter-Sessions, may also tax every Parish in the County towards Relief of Prisoners for Debt in the common Gaol, so as it does not exceed 6d. or 8d. a Week for every Parish, to be levied by Church-wardens, and paid once a Quarter to the High Constables or Head Officers of every Town, *etc.* who are to pay it to the Collectors appointed by the Justices in their Sessions. *Stat. 14 El. c.5.*

Justices in their Sessions may likewise provide a sufficient Stock to set poor Prisoners to work, committed for Felony, and other Misdemeanors, by such Ways and Means as other County-Charges are raised, provided no Parish be rated above 6d. a Week; and they may appoint Overseers and Collectors, examine their Accounts, and punish Abuses, *etc. Stat. 19 Car.2. c.4.*

Many People being poor by Losses, and other Misfortunes, and not able to make Satisfaction to their Creditors; the Statutes *22 & 23 Car.2.; 2 W. & M.; 1 Ann.; 6 Geo.1.; 2 Geo.2. etc.* enacted, that if a poor Man was in Prison for Debt, he might petition a Justice, *etc.* who by Warrant was to require the Gaoler to bring the Prisoner to the Quarter-Sessions, together with a Copy of the Cause of his Commitment; and the Prisoner in the Sessions delivering up a Schedule of his whole Estate, and the Names of his Creditors, and the several Sums of Money due to them, and making Oath that he was not worth £10 he should be discharged.

But no Person was to have the Benefit of the Acts who owed more than £50

Principal and Interest, to any one Person.

Poor Apprentices.

The placing forth of poor Children Apprentices, is esteemed one of the best Methods of providing for the Poor.

Church-wardens and Overseers of the Poor may put out Children of Parents not able to maintain them; but it must be by the Assent of two Justices.

The Children so put forth are to be above Seven, and under Fifteen Years of Age; and those above the Age of Ten Years, may be bound by their own Agreement, by Indenture, *etc.* and if above Twelve, they may be compelled by a Justice. And the Man-child shall be bound 'till he come to the Age of Twenty-four, and the Woman-child 'till Twenty-one. *Dalt. 143.; Stat. 43 Eliz. c.2.*

Church-wardens and Overseers, with the Assistance of the Justices, may oblige all Persons of Ability, as Gentlemen, Clergymen, Yeomen and Tradesmen, (such as Bakers, Brewers, Carpenters, Masons, Weavers, Taylors, Dyers, Fullers, *etc.*) to take Apprentices, either with Money, or without, there being no Necessity of giving Money with them; for it is discretionary in the Church-wardens, whether they will give any or not. And Justices shall determine Disagreements between Masters and Officers.

Overseers of the Poor are Judges of the Disability of Parents to maintain their Children; and such as refuse to have their Children placed forth Apprentice, may be bound over to the Sessions: Children refusing to be bound, are to be sent to the House of Correction, 'till they shall be willing. *Dalt.148, 153.*

Masters refusing to receive such Apprentices by the Stat. *43 Eliz. c.2.* were to be bound over to the Assizes; and if they refused to give Bond, they might be committed; or the Church-wardens and Overseers, by the Consent of two Justices, had Power to fine them to raise Money to place the Apprentices with others; and if they refused to pay such Fines, the two Justices might make a Warrant to levy them by Distress, *etc.* But now by the Statute *8 & 9 W.3. c.30.* upon the Church-wardens making Oath of the Refusal of the Master, before two Justices, he forfeits £10 to be levied by Warrant of the two Justices, to the Use of the Poor.

Though the Party may appeal to the next Sessions; and a Man may not be compelled to take an Apprentice that may be a Spy on his Family; a Thief, Enemy, *etc. Vent. Rep.325.*

Monies may be raised for placing out Apprentices by Overseers, in like Manner as for Relief of Poor, by taxing every Inhabitant, and Occupier of Lands, Houses, Tithes, *etc.. Stat. 7 Jac.1.* And where Charity-Money is given for that Purpose, if in Towns Corporate, it shall be employed by the Corporation; if in other Places, by the Parson, Constable, Church-wardens and Overseers, *etc.* or the greater Part of them; who if they refuse, forfeit five Marks each, to the Use of the Poor. *Stat. 7 Jac.1. c.3.*

Masters must give Security to repay what Money they take with such an Apprentice, at the End of Seven Years, or within one Year after the Death of the Apprentice, if he die in that Time; to be employed for putting out others. The Trustees must account in *Easter* Week, to the two next Justices.

If there be no fit Persons to be Apprentices in the Place where the Money is given, it may be employed in the Parishes adjoining; but the Church-wardens cannot place them to Masters in another Parish, tho' the Justices in Sessions may; and if there are no Masters fit to receive them in the Hundred, then they may be put out in the County at large by Order of Sessions.

Apprentices may be placed to Farmers, who shall receive them for Husbandry; and single Women, Widows, *etc.* for Housewifry, *etc.* But Apprentices in Husbandry must be above the Age of ten, and under eighteen. They may serve till twenty-one, or twenty-four Years of Age; and Justices of Peace may compel Persons that are fit, to serve in Husbandry as Apprentices, until one and twenty. *Stat. 5 Eliz.*

An Indenture of Apprenticeship.

This *Indenture* made, *etc.* between *A.B.* and *C.D.* Church-wardens of the Parish of, *etc.* in the County of, *etc.* and *E.F.* and *G.H.* Overseers of the Poor of the same Parish, of the one Part, and *J.K.* of, *etc.* Taylor, of the other Part, *Witnesseth*, That the said Church-wardens and Overseers, by the Assent of, *etc.* two of his Majesty's Justices of Peace of the said County, according to the Direction of the Statute made in the forty-third Year of the Reign of Queen *Elizabeth* for the Relief of the Poor, hath put out and bound *L.M.* a poor Child of the Parish of, *etc.* (or Son of, *etc.* who is not able to bring up and maintain him) Apprentice to the said *J.K.* 'till the said *L.M.* shall come to the Age of twenty-four Years. During all which Time, the said Apprentice his said Master well and faithfully shall serve, his Secrets keep, his lawful Commands every where willingly do. He shall do no Hurt or Damage to his said Master, nor consent to its being done by others, but shall forthwith give Notice thereof: He shall not waste the Goods of his said Master; nor lend them to any Person without his Consent. He shall not frequent Taverns, nor Alehouses, during the said Term (except it be in his Master's Business) and he shall not play at Cards, Dice, or other unlawful Games. He shall not, either by Day or Night, absent himself from his said Master's Service, but in all Things as a good and faithful Servant, shall demean himself towards his said Master, and all his. And the said *J.K.* his said Apprentice shall, during the said Term, educate and bring up, or cause to be educated and brought up, in his Trade of a Taylor in the best Manner that he can; and find and allow unto him during the said Term sufficient, wholesome and competent Meat, Drink, Lodging, Washing, Apparel, and all other Necessaries meet for such an Apprentice. *In Witness, etc.*

The Consent of the Justices indorsed on the Backside.

We whose Names are hereunto subscribed, Justices of the Peace of the County of, *etc.* do consent to the putting forth *L.M.* Apprentice according to the Intent and Meaning of the within written Indenture. *J.L. T.J.*

To these Indentures, it is sometimes usual to add a Clause for the Master at the End of the Term to provide for his Apprentice two Suits of Apparel; one for *Sundays*, and the other for working Days: And Masters may not take away Apparel from Apprentices, tho' they part with them. *Bro.Tres.93.*

Mayors, Bailiffs, or other Head Officers of Corporate Towns, have in their several Precincts like Authority, as the Justices of Peace have in Counties, for all the Uses and Purposes in this Act: And so hath every Alderman of a Ward in the City of *London. Stat. 43 Eliz. c.2.*

Justices may discharge an Apprentice; and order a Restitution of Money given where the Fault is in the Master, as Negligence in instructing his Apprentice in his Trade, not allowing him Necessaries, beating him unreasonably, *etc. Hawksworth's Case, 25 Car.2.; Keb.6.* If the Fault be in the Apprentice, he may be sent to the House of Correction, by *Stat. 5 Eliz. c.4.*

Lessee for Years of a Farm takes an Apprentice, and the Term expires before the Apprenticeship is ended, he must go with the Farm, if his Master will permit him; but where a Man taketh an Apprentice by Reason of his Ability, and the Master dies before the End of the Apprenticeship, he shall go to the Executor or Administrator, if he hath Assets; and if none, then he must return to the Parish where last settled. *Shew. Rep.405.*

Besides the Statutes aforementioned relating to Apprentices, the Stat. *2 Ann.* requires the placing forth poor Apprentices to the Sea-Service.

Two Justices, Mayors, or chief Magistrates of Towns, *etc.* or Church-wardens and Overseers of the Poor, with the Consent of two Justices, *etc.* may place out Boys of ten Years of Age, and upwards, (by an Act since made, 13) likely to be a Charge on the Parish, whose Parents are chargeable; and those who beg for Alms, to the Sea-Service, till they come to the Age of one and twenty Years; and £2 10s. is to be given with each Boy by the Church-wardens and Overseers, to provide Clothing and Bedding, which will be allowed in their Accounts. *2 Ann. c.6.* Boys are to be sent to the Port likewise at the Charge of the Parish, in the same Manner as Vagrants. *11 & 12 W.3.*

Every Master or Owner of a Ship from 30 to 50 Tuns, not taking one such poor Boy Apprentice; one more for the next 50 Tuns, and one more for every 100 Tuns above the first 100, shall forfeit £10 to the Poor of the Parish from whence the Boy was to be bound. *Stat. 2 Ann. c.6.*

Church-wardens are to send the Counterpart of the Indenture to the Collector of the Customs, in the Port to which the Master belongs; it must be sealed by the Master, in the Presence of the Collector and Constable there, and be attested by them, and afterwards returned to the Church-wardens: But such Collector must first enter it in a Book, and indorse on the Indenture that 'tis registred, and subscribe his Name without Fee, or he shall be liable to the Penalty of £5 to the Use of the Poor. *Ibid. Stat.*

Collectors at their Ports are to keep a Register of the Names of Masters and Apprentices, and from what Parishes they came; the Number and Burden of all Ships and Vessels, *etc.* and transmit true Copies thereof to the Quarter-Sessions when thereunto required.

These Apprentices shall not be pressed, till they are 18 Years of Age; but then they may be pressed, and the Masters shall receive their Wages.

Parish Boys bound Apprentice, according to *43 Eliz.* may at the Request of the Master, *etc.* and with the Consent of two Justices, be turned over to Masters and Owners of Ships, for the remaining Time of their Apprenticeships, by Indenture of Assignment: And the Widows of Masters of Ships may assign over their poor Apprentices to other Masters. In other Cases, a poor Child bound Apprentice, cannot be legally assigned to another Master. *1 Salk.68.*

Two Justices, *etc.* near the Port where any Vessel shall arrive, have Power to hear and determine all Complaints of hard Usage to these Apprentices; and to make Orders as between Masters and Servants. *Stat. 2 Ann. cap.6.*

The Assignment of an Apprentice, tho' with his consent, will not make him an Apprentice to the Assignee, within the Stat. *5 Eliz. c.4.* But in the City of *London*, by the Custom, such Assignment is good. *3 Keb.519.*

Justices of Peace have Conusance of Apprentices bound by private Persons, as well as by Overseers of the Poor: And Justices may discharge such an Apprentice, if the Fault be in the Master. The Justices cannot punish a bad Master, tho' they may discharge the Apprentice; and may punish a bad Apprentice, *etc.*

On Complaint of an Apprentice, one Justice is to bind the Master over to the next general Sessions, and four Justices there are to discharge the Apprentice; and upon Complaint of the Master, to send the Apprentice to the House of Correction, if he will not appear at the Sessions, and abide the Order of the Justices. *Skinn.98.*

An Action of Trespass will lie for taking an Apprentice out of his actual Service; and for enticing him out of the Master's Service, or to take Money or Play, or detaining a hired Servant, an Action of the Case will give Remedy. *Noy 105.*

By *5 Eliz.* none shall set up any Trade who hath not served 7 Years Apprenticeship; but Apprentices going into the Army might do it in the County where born, by *Stat. 10 & 11 W.3.*

Of Servants, etc.

Two Justices of Peace, Mayors or other Head Officers of any City, Borough or Town Corporate, may warn all single Persons under the Age of thirty, to go to Service at a Time prefixed; and any Woman upwards of twelve, and under forty Years old, being unmarried, they may compel to go to Service.

If such Persons neglect to go to Service, and continue to live idly, having no visible Estate, they may be sent to the House of Correction, or be bound over to the Sessions, and to be of the Good Behaviour in the mean Time. *Stat. 5 Eliz. cap.4.*

Justices of the Peace in their *Easter*-Sessions, or within six Weeks after, Mayors, *etc.* are to limit and assess the Wages of Servants, Labourers, Workmen, *etc.* on Pain of £10. Every Justice being absent, and not having some reasonable Excuse. *Stat. 5 Eliz. cap.4.* Labourers and Workmen working by the Day, Week, Month or Year, or taking Work by the Great, are within the Statute; and Sheriffs and Mayors, *etc.* are to proclaim the Rates. *Stat. 1 Jac.1. cap.6.*

If Justices in Sessions make an Order for the Payment of Servants Wage, it is good, by Reason they have Power to compel the Service; but for the Wages of a Coachman, or the like, they have no Power to make an Order, because they cannot oblige a Man to serve in that Capacity. And one *Ryecroft*, a *Middlesex* Justice, had £30 Damages recovered against him for making an Order for the Payment of a Seaman's Wages. *T. Jones's Rep.47.*

If a Master gives more Wages than set by Justices, he forfeits £5 and may be committed for ten Days without Bail: And a Servant taking more Wages, shall be committed for one and twenty Days: But a Master may reward a Servant as he pleases, so as it is not by Way of Contract on the Retainer. *Stat. 5 Eliz. c.4.*

If a Labourer or Servant depart before he has finished his Work agreed to be performed (except for Non-payment of Wages, or with Leave of the Master, or being taken into the King's Service) he is to be committed for a Month without Bail, and to forfeit £5. *Stat. 5 Eliz. c.4.*

If a Servant refuse to serve for the Wages appointed by Justices; or having promised to serve, shall not comply, he shall be committed until he gives Security for his Service; and if a Servant depart before the End of his Term, being hired for a Year, without Cause allowed by a Justice, or after his Term is expired, without giving a Quarter's Warning, two Justices may commit him without Bail, till he give Security to serve for the Time agreed on. *Stat. 5 Eliz.* And by the Statute *7 Jac.1. c.4.* one Justice may send him to the House of Correction, there to be punished as a disorderly Person.

A Master likewise cannot put away a Servant before the End of his Term, without some reasonable Cause, to be allowed by one Justice; nor after the End of the Term, without a Quarter's Warning given before Witness; if a Master discharges a Servant otherwise, he is liable to a Penalty of 40s. *Stat. 5 Eliz. cap.6.*

A Servant ought not to be discharged by Reason of Sickness, or any other Disability by the Act of God; nor may his Wages be abated for those Causes. *Dalt.129.*

But both Master and Servant may part by Consent; and then the Allowance of the Cause by a Justice of Peace is not necessary. A Master's detaining Wages, or not allowing sufficient Meat, Drink, *etc.* is good Cause for a Servant's Departure; but it must be allowed by a Justice. *Dalt.*

If a Master puts away his Servant, he shall have Wages to the Time he served; but if the Servant depart himself before the End of his Time, he loses all his Wages.

If a Servant be retained a Year, according to the Statute, and the Master dieth within that Time, the Executors must pay the Wages; *Contra*, if the Retainer was not for a Year. But all Retainers and Promises for Payment of Wages, contrary to the Statute, are void. *Stat. 5 Eliz. cap.4.*

A Servant or Workman assaulting his Master, may be bound to the Good Behaviour by one Justice; or two Justices may commit him for a Year or less at their Discretion. *5 Eliz.* And if any Servant shall purloin or make away with his Master's Goods to the Value of 40s. it is Felony. *Stat. 12 Ann.*

If a Woman with Child procure herself to be retained with a Master who knows nothing thereof, this is good Cause to discharge her from her Service; if she be gotten with Child during her Service, it is the same Thing; and if the Term be ended, or she lawfully discharged, the Master is not bound to provide for her; but 'tis a Misfortune laid upon the Parish, which they must bear as in Cases of casual Impotency. Resolved *Anno* 1633.

The Master not having legally discharged his House of such a Servant, he must provide for her till her Delivery, and one Month after; and then she is to be sent to the Place where last legally settled. *Dalt.*

If a Woman Servant marrieth, she is obliged to serve out her Time; and if both Man and Wife agree to serve, they must perform the Agreement. *Dalt.92.*

An Agreement between a Master and a Servant.

Memorandum. It is agreed this Day, *etc.* between *A.B.* and *C.D.* in Manner following, *viz.* That he the said *A.B.* shall and will receive the said *C.D.* into his

House and Service for the Term of one whole Year, from the Date hereof; and provide for the said *C.D.* competent and sufficient Meat, Drink, Washing and Lodging; and also pay and allow unto him the said *C.D.* the Sum or Wages of £5 he the said *C.D.* continuing in the Service of him the said *A.B.* during the said Term: *And* the said *C.D.* covenants and agrees with the said *A.B.* That he the said *C.D.* shall and will for the Considerations aforesaid, faithfully serve him the said *A.B.* in the Business and Service of, *etc.* for and during the said Term of one Year, without absenting from the same, or imbezilling any of the Money or Goods of the said *A.B.*or any Ways disclosing the Secrets of his said Master. *In Witness* whereof the Parties aforesaid have hereunto set their Hands, *etc.* the Day and Year above written.

Of Bastards.

As Bastards are frequently chargeable to Parishes; I shall take some Notice of them.

All Children born out of lawful Wedlock, are Bastards: And Issue born before Marriage, tho' the Parties afterwards intermarry: Issue by a second Wife, the first living; the Issue of Persons divorced; Children born during Marriage, where a Husband is gelt; Children born after a Husband has been some Years beyond the Sea, or not within the four Seas during the Woman's being with Child, are likewise Bastards. *47 Ed.3.; 18 H.6.; Co. Litt.235.; Roll. Abr.358, etc.*

But Issue born forty Weeks and eight Days after the Departure or Death of the Husband, is no Bastard. *Cro. 1 Jac. 451. Alsop* vers. *Bowtrell.* Though *Coke* upon *Littleton* holds forty Weeks to be the latest Time for the Birth of legitimate Issue, *p.123.*

Where a Bastard is begotten on a Woman, she is to be examined upon Oath by a Justice of Peace; and on her Swearing to the reputed Father, the Justice shall issue out his Warrant for his Apprehension; and when the Person appears before the Justice, he is to enter into Recognizance with Sureties, and to be of the Good Behaviour, 'till Order be made by two Justices. *Dalt.39.; 1 Salk.380.*

The Examination of a Woman with Child of a Bastard.

Midd. ss. The Examination of *E.B.* single Woman, taken before me *T.D.* Esq. one of his Majesty's Justices of Peace for the said County, this Day and Year, *etc.* who on her Oath saith, that she is a hired Servant to *M.F.* of, *etc.* and that in the Month of *May* last, as she this Examinant was making one of her Master's Beds, in, *etc.* Room of his House, *A.T.* a Mercer, living the next Door, came into the said Room, no other Person being present, and promising great Kindness to this Examinant, prevail'd with her, and then had the carnal Knowledge of her Body, once on the said Bed, and hath had the same three several Times since; and that at one of the said Times, he the said *A.T.* got her with a Bastard-Child, with which she is now pregnant, and near the Time of her Delivery: And this Examinant further upon Oath saith, that he the said *A.T.* is the only true Father of the said Bastard, with which she is now pregnant, as aforesaid; or of which she was delivered on, *etc.* (If after Delivery). *Sworn the Day and Year aforesaid, before   E.B.   T.D.*

When the Child is born, two Justices (*Quorum unus*) who are next the Place, are at a private Meeting to examine the Matter, and make an Order for the punishing the Father and Mother, the Relief of the Parish in Part, or in all, and charging the Parents with Payment of Money weekly, for Maintenance of the Child: But a Bastard of a Person able to keep it, and not likely to become chargeable to the Parish, is not within the Statute. *Stat. 18 Eliz. cap.3.*

Justices have no Power but to indemnify the Parish; that is, only to oblige the putative Father to maintain the Child as long as it is, or may be, chargeable to the Parish; for the Father may take the Child when he pleases, and maintain it himself; wherefore Orders for Payment of Money weekly, 'till the Child attains a certain Age, have been quashed. *2 Saund. 82.; 1 Salk.121, etc.*

Altho' none but the Justices of Peace have Power to adjudge who is the putative Father of a Bastard-Child; yet if the Justices are unreasonable in appointing Provision for the Child, as if they appoint but 2d. a Week, *etc.* the Court of *B.R.* will judge of that. *2 Sid.361.*

In the Drawing of Orders in these Cases; the Order must be concerning a Bastard, and so expressed; it must contain a positive Adjudication who is the reputed Father; and that the Child is likely to become chargeable to the Parish; the Justices may Order the Father or Mother to maintain the Child, and no other Person; one of the Justices must be of the *Quorum*, and both at the Time they make their Order in the County for which they are Justices; it must appear by the Order, that they are the Justices next to the Parish where the Bastard-Child is born; and that the Child was born in the Parish, to which the Money is ordered to be paid. *Style 154.; 1 Vent.37, 310.; Cro. Car.213.; 1 Keb.383.*

An Order of Justices for maintaining a Bastard-Child.

Whereas M.A. was on or about, *etc.* last past delivered of a Bastard-Child in the Parish of, *etc.* which is now living, and likely to become chargeable to the said Parish: *And whereas,* upon due Examination, it appears, that *A.B.* of, *etc.* is the Father of the said Bastard Child. *Now* we *T.D.* and *J.S.* of, *etc.* Esqrs; two of his Majesty's Justices of Peace for the County aforesaid, and living nearest to the said Parish of, *etc.* For the Relief of the said Parish, and Maintenance of the said Bastard-Child, do according to the Statutes in that Case made and provided, Order the said *A.B.* to pay weekly and every Week from the Time of the Birth of the said Child, and so long as it shall be chargeable to the said Parish of, *etc.* unto the Church-wardens or Overseers of the Poor of the said Parish for the Time being, the Sum of, *etc.* for and towards the Maintenance of the said Child: *And* we do hereby further order, That the said *M.A.* shall pay weekly, and every Week, for so long Time as the said Child shall be chargeable to the said Parish of, *etc.* as aforesaid, and she shall not keep the same, the Sum of, *etc.* to the Church-wardens, *etc.* of the said Parish for the Time being, for the further Maintenance of the said Child: *Or,* that she the said *M.A.* shall be sent to the House of Correction, and there kept to hard Labour, *etc.* (If she be not able to contribute to the Maintenance of the Child.) *And lastly,* we order, That the said *A.B. etc.* do upon Notice of this our Order, forthwith give sufficient Security to the Church-wardens and Overseers of the said Parish of, *etc.* well and truly to do and perform what is ordered as aforesaid. *In Witness, etc.*

The putative Father may appeal to the Order at the next Sessions, if he hath good Cause: And upon the Appeal, the Sessions will either affirm or quash the Order of the two Justices: And in Case the two Justices cannot agree in making their Order, it may be referr'd to the Sessions. If the reputed Father brings an Appeal against the Order, he must enter into a Recognizance for his Appearance at the Sessions, to have the Matter determin'd: Not giving Security to the Parish, and refusing to enter into such Recognizance, the two Justices making the Order, may commit him. *Stat. 18 Eliz.*

If Justices of Peace in their Sessions, revoke an Order of two Justices for keeping a Bastard-Child; and no Father can be found, they are liable to keep the Child themselves. *Vent.59.*

If a Child dies after the Order is made, and before the next Sessions, and no Security be given to perform the Order; yet when the Party appears at the Sessions, the Justices may order him to pay the Charges, upon Proof of serving the Order.

And an Order made to pay such Charges as the Parish had been at, without saying, that the Child was likely to be chargeable, *etc.* was held good. *1 Vent.37.*

By a late Statute, a single Woman deliver'd of a Bastard in any Parish or extraparochial Place, or declaring her self to be with Child; on Oath before a Justice, charging any Person with getting it, he may issue his Warrant to apprehend the reputed Father, to give Security to appear at the next Sessions, and perform Orders made; and not doing it, may commit him to the House of Correction, *etc.*

But if such Woman die, or be married, or if she miscarry, or it happens she was not with Child; or if no Order be made in six Weeks after her Delivery, the Man shall be discharged by the Justices: And no Justice may compel any Woman before delivered, and one Month after, to answer Questions. *Stat. 6 Geo.2. c.31.*

If the Father of a Bastard-Child pay a competent Sum of Money in Gross to the Overseers of the Poor, for Maintenance of the Child, he shall be discharged; and the Overseers are to release him: But if he do not pay such a Sum, he may give Bond to the Church-wardens and Overseers, to indemnify the Parish; and if the Child then become chargeable to the Parish, the Justices may not intermeddle; but the Parish must sue the Sureties on the Bond.

A Condition of a Bond given to Church-wardens and Overseers of the Poor, for indemnifying the Parish from a Bastard-Child.

Whereas, M.A. of, *etc.* Single Woman, upon Examination lately taken before, *etc.* one of his Majesty's Justices of the Peace for the County of, *etc.* aforesaid, hath declared and affirmed upon Oath, that she is great with Child, (or hath been lately delivered of a Bastard-Child,) And that the above-bound *A.B.* is the Father of such Child or Children she now goeth withal. *And whereas* the said Child or Children when born, may become chargeable to the Parish of, *etc.* aforesaid: *If therefore* the said *A.B.* and the above-bound *E.F.* and *G.H.* or either or any of them, their, or either or any of their Heirs, Executors, or Administrators, do and shall from Time to Time, and at all Times hereafter, fully and clearly exonerate and discharge, or otherwise well and sufficiently save and keep harmless and indemnify, as well the above-named *J.K. L.M.* and *N.O.* Church-wardens and Overseers of the Poor of the Parish of, *etc.* aforesaid, and their Successors for the Time being, and every of them; as also all the Inhabitants and Parishioners of the said Parish of, *etc.* which now are, or hereafter shall be, and every of them of and from all manner of Expences, Damages, Costs and Charges whatsoever, which shall or may at any Time hereafter arise, happen, come, grow, or be imposed upon them, or either, or any of them, for or by Reason or Means of the said *M.A.*'s being now great with Child as aforesaid; or for or by Reason and Means of the Birth, Maintenance, Education, and bringing up of such Child or Children that she the said *A.B.* now goeth with; and of and from all other Troubles, Charges, Damages and Demands whatsoever concerning the same; then, *etc.* or else, *etc.*

If the Party do not give such a Bond of Indemnity, the two Justices are to proceed in the making of their Order, for the Security of the Parish; and if after the Order made, the reputed Father and Mother having Notice thereof, shall not perform the same, the Party making Default shall be committed 'till Security be given for the Performance of the Order, or to appear at the next Quarter-Sessions. *Stat. 18 Eliz. c.3.*

Church-wardens and Overseers of the Poor where a Bastard shall be born, may by Order of two Justices seize Goods, and receive Rents of the Lands of the reputed Father and lewd Mother towards the Discharge of the Parish; which Order being confirmed in the Sessions, the Church-wardens may sell the Goods, *etc. Stat. 24 Car.2. c.12.* Though this is seldom done but where a Party withdraws himself clandestinely.

Two Justices may inflict a corporal Punishment upon the reputed Father, not being of Ability to discharge the Parish, by Whipping. *Stat. 18 Eliz. c.3.* And by the Statute *7 Jac.1.* the Justices may commit lewd Women to the House of Correction, who have Bastards that may be chargeable to the Parish, there to be punished and set at Work for a Year.

But if the Woman will discharge the Parish, she cannot be punished by this last Act; yet, by Virtue of *18 Eliz.* she may be punished by Whipping: But a Woman is not to receive any Punishment 'till she is deliver'd. *Dalt.41.*

Officers negligently suffering an Escape of the reputed Father, and any Person who shall persuade or convey away the reputed Father or Mother, may be bound over to the Sessions by one Justice, and there be ordered to contribute towards the Maintenance of the Child. But it hath been held in a late Case, that the Justices have no Authority to do this; though such Persons may be indicted and fined. *Mich. 11 Ann. B.R.*

Justices in Corporations, *etc.* are to put the Acts in Execution relating to Bastardy as Justices in the Counties, *etc.* And it is Murder for a Woman to conceal the Death of her Bastard. *3 Car.1. c.4.; 21 Jac.1.*

If any Person shall conspire to charge another with a Bastard-Child, he may be indicted; and a Woman wrongly charging a Man with getting a Bastard upon her Body, was committed to the House of Correction for Life. *Pasch. 13 Car.1.* The usual Punishment of these Offenders, is publick Whipping, *etc. 1 Vent.305.*

Bastards, having in the Eye of the Law no Father, gain a Settlement by their Birth. They are to be placed with their Mother till Seven Years of Age; and then be sent to their Place of Birth, the Mother or reputed Father not being able to provide for them.

Of Settlements.

We have several Laws in Force to confine Men to certain Places of Settlement, and Habitation; and by Statute, every Parish is obliged to provide for its own Poor. *43 Eliz. cap.2.*

If a Father has a legal Settlement in a Parish, the Child is settled where the Father is; but if the Father has no legal Settlement, then the Child gains a Settlement in the Parish where born. *2 Bulst.351.*

If Parents of poor Children die wandering and *in Transitu*, the Children are to be provided for by the Parish where they were born; for the Place of Birth is a certain Settlement, and Parents wandering with them afterwards will not alter the Case. *Bulstr. Rep.351.*

Children shall be sent to, and settled with the Parents: And Children above Seven Years of Age, found begging, and vagrant with the Parents, are to be sent to *Bridewell* with them; if under, to the Place where they last passed through without Punishment.

If a Woman with Child sent to the House of Correction, be there delivered, the Child shall not gain a Settlement in the Parish where born; but the Parish where the Mother dwelled when sent to the House of Correction, shall provide for the Child. *2 Bulstr.358.*

If a travelling Woman, having a small Child sucking on her, is apprehended for Felony, and tried, condemned, and executed, this Child is to be sent to the Place of its Birth, if that can be known; if not, to the Place where the Mother was taken. *Dalt.158.*

'Till Seven Years of Age, Children are accounted Nurse-Children. If a poor Man settled at *A.* marries a poor Woman who is settled at *B.* and has Children by a former Husband, the Wife shall be sent with him to *A.* and also the Children under Seven Years old, but only for Nurture; so that they shall be kept at the Charge of the Parish from whence removed: And the Children above Seven Years of Age are not removeable. *2 Salk.470, 482.*

A Wife is to be sent to, and settled with her Husband; and tho' he be at a Place but as an Inmate or Servant, she shall be settled with him: But if a Husband hath a House in one Parish, and live there by Night, and is a Covenant Servant to a Master in another Parish, where he is all the Day; in this Case his Wife and Children shall continue in the first Place, where they are settled; tho' if the Husband take a House in the last Parish, they must be settled there with him. *Dalt.*

The Law unsettles none who are lawfully settled; nor permits it to be done by Compulsion, *etc.* A Man having a Wife and Children, takes a House in the Parish of *B.* for a Year; and in that Year he is wrongfully turned out of Possession; whereupon he takes a House in the Parish of *C.* from which he is also ejected in a short Space; and thereby wanting a Place to live in, he gets in a Barn in the Parish of *D.* and there his Wife is delivered of another Child; in this Case they are all to be sent to the Parish of *B.* out of which they were first illegally forced. *Resol.*1633.

If any Person by indirect Means, hinder a poor Man from hiring a House, he may for such Disturbance, be indicted. It is fineable to remove or put any out of the Parish, who ought not to be put out; and the Persons so removed may be conveyed back. *Dalt. 98.*

If a Man have an Estate in a Parish, he cannot be remov'd from thence though he is likely to become chargeable, let him be settled where he will. *5 Mod.419.* but see Statute *9 Geo.1. c.7.* And Persons whose Interest in Houses or Lands is determined, cannot be put out of the Town where legally settled, but they shall be relieved or set on Work there; unless they commit any Act of Vagrancy, when they may be sent to the Place of their Birth. *Dalt.158.*

The Statutes relating to Settlements, are the *13 & 14 Car.2.; 3 & 4 W.& M.; 8 & 9 W.3.; 12 Ann. etc.* By the Statute *13 & 14 Car.2. c.12.* when any poor Person came to settle in a Parish in a Tenement under £10 *per Ann.* upon Complaint by the Church-wardens and Overseers of the Poor to any Justice of Peace within 40 Days, two Justices might by Order remove him to the Place where he last dwelt for 40 Days; which shews that 40 Days made a Settlement before this Act.

But the 40 Days were to be accounted from the Time of publick Notice given to the Church-wardens or Overseers in Writing of the Place of his Abode, and Number of his Family; and their publishing of it likewise. *Stat. 3 & 4 W.& M.*

This Notice was to be read in the Church by the Overseers or Church-wardens, the next *Sunday* after Divine Service, under the Penalty of 40s. The like Penalty for neglecting to register such Notice, to be levied by Distress, *etc.* And for want of Distress, to be committed for a Month without Bail. *Stat. Ibid.*

But Persons renting £10 a Year, executing upon their own Account any publick yearly Office, or Charge for a Year, paying to the Poor's Rate, or any Share of Taxes of the Parish, (unless it be the King's Tax;) unmarried Persons not having Children, hired as Servants for a Year; and Persons bound Apprentice, and inhabiting in a Town, are excepted out of this Act, and gain a Settlement without giving Notice as aforesaid. *Stat. 3 & 4 W.& M. c.11.*

A Person Rents two Tenements of £5 *per Ann.* each, he thereby gains a Settlement: But if a Man Rent a Piece of Land of £10 *per Ann.* and there is no House belonging to it, it is otherwise. *Hill.1710.* In Case a Person Rents £14 a Year, but it lies in two Parishes; it makes a Settlement where he resides.

By *Parker* Chief Justice, Renting a Tenement of £10 a Year, for a Month, is a fraudulent Renting; but if one Rents a House of £10 *per Ann.* and continues forty Days, he gains a Settlement, within the Meaning of *13 & 14 Car.2.*

A Man who is chose Parish Clerk by the Parson, and receives his Fees and Duties, it is a Parish Office; and if they let him continue a Year, none can remove him and his Family. *Mich.1711.*

In respect to Servants, it must be one entire Hiring, and one entire Year's Service, in Pursuance of that Hiring, that can gain the Party a Settlement, by Force of the Act *3 & 4 W.& M.*

A Servant was hired from *Lady-Day* to *Michaelmas*, and then to *Lady-Day* following; adjudged a good Settlement, there being an entire Hiring for a Year, though different Times are mentioned. *Hill. 10 W.3.*

An unmarried Person hired for a Year, married before the Year was expired; and it was held, that he could not be removed, and that upon performing his Service he would gain a Settlement. *2 Salk.527.*

And if a Maid Servant hired for a Year, be turned away on Account of Sickness before the Year expired, she nevertheless obtains a Settlement there. *Style 168*.

A Servant being hired at *A*. for a Year, his Master lives there Half a Year, and then lives at *B*. another Half-year; adjudged the Servant is settled in the last Place; for the Statute doth not tie the Service down to one Place.

A Person is a Lodger in a Parish, yet his Servant acquires a Settlement: And Servants to Lodgers and Visitors, gain a Settlement in the Parish where they continue to serve *etc. Mod. Cas. L. & E. 50*.

An Apprentice bound to one who is a Lodger only in a Parish, and hath no Settlement; *per Cur.* the Apprentice is well settled there, altho' the Master is not; nor does his Settlement depend upon his Master, as that of a Wife on her Husband. *Parish of St*. Brides.

When a Person is bound Apprentice by Indenture, where-ever he continues forty Days in the Service of his Master, there such Apprentice gains a Settlement; and where any Person serves the last forty Days of his Apprenticeship, that is the Place of his last legal Settlement. *Hill. 4 Ann. B.R.*

An Apprentice served two Years in one Parish, and was by Agreement turned over to a Master in another Parish, and there serv'd out his Time: This was held a good Settlement in that other Parish where he last serv'd. *Trin. 9 Geo.1.*

No Settlement can be legal in any Parish, when the Residence of the Party is obscure, and uncertain; or where a Person is under Disturbance by Officers. *3 & 4 W. & M.*

By the Statute *8 & 9 W.3. c.30.* a poor Man may remove from one Parish to another, having a Certificate under the Hands and Seals of the Church-wardens and Overseers of the Poor, or under the Hands and Seals of the Overseers, where there are no Church-wardens, acknowledging the Person therein mentioned to be an Inhabitant legally settled in their Parish; which Certificate being attested by two Witnesses, and allowed and subscribed by two Justices, shall oblige the Parish to receive the Person, *etc.* when he shall become chargeable, *etc.*

But no Person who shall come with such Certificate shall have a legal Settlement in the Parish, unless he *bona fide* take a Lease of a Tenement of £10 *per Annum*, or shall be placed in, and execute some annual Office. *Stat. 9 & 10 W.3. c.11.*

And he who shall be an Apprentice by Indenture, or a hired Servant to one who comes into a Parish by Certificate, not afterwards gaining a legal Settlement there, shall not by Virtue of his Apprenticeship, Indenture, or binding, nor such Servant, by being hired or serving such Person, gain any Settlement there. *12 Ann. c.18.*

A Certificate of a Person's being a Parishioner.

We whose Names are here under-written, Church-wardens and Overseers of the Poor of the Parish of, *etc.* in the County aforesaid, do certify that *A.B.* Labourer, the Bearer hereof, is an Inhabitant legally settled in our said Parish of, *etc.* And we do hereby oblige ourselves and Successors, to receive the said *A.B.* and his Family, whenever he shall become chargeable to the Parish of, *etc.* by Impotency, Casualty, Sickness, or otherwise; to which said Parish of, *etc.* the said *A.B.* is desirous to remove for his better Support and Employment. *In Witness* whereof, we have hereunto set our Hands and Seals, *etc.*

    C.D. Church-warden.   *E.F.* & G.H.   Overseers.   *J.K.* & L.M. Inhabitants.

    We *N.O.* and *W.R.* Esqs; two of his Majesty's Justices of the Peace for the County of, *etc.* aforesaid, do hereby allow of the Certificate above-mention'd. *Witness* our Hands,   *N.O.*   *W.R.*

    N. B. The Act *3 Geo.2.* requires an *Oath*, by Witnesses, of the Signing of Certificates; and Justices to *certify* the same. Vide *Post.*

    Some Years since a Question arose between two Parishes, in the County of *Northampton*, upon an Order remov'd into *B.R.* which was thus: A Person who was not legally settled in the Parish, but had lived there some Time, procured a Certificate, by Virtue of which he went into another Parish, where he was as an Inhabitant with them; afterwards being Poor, the Parish from whence he came took him again; but upon Enquiry found that he was never lawfully settled with them, but had gain'd a Settlement in another Place, before they gave this Certificate; and thither they remov'd him by Order. The Parish to which he was remov'd appeal'd, because those who had given the Certificate, had owned him to be an Inhabitant settled with them; but the Certificate was held by the Court to be only an Evidence of a Settlement; and thereupon the first Order was confirmed. *Trin. 2 Ann.; 2 Salk.530.*

    But it was adjudg'd *Mich. 9 Ann.* That a Certificate concludes the Parish giving it, not only against the Parish to which it is given, but as to all other Parishes; it being a solemn Acknowledgment and Adjudication. *Ibid. 535.*

    Church-wardens and Overseers refusing to receive a Person sent by Order of two Justices, forfeit £5 to the Use of the Poor of the Parish from whence the Party was removed. *Stat. 12 Ann. c.18.*

    But though they may not refuse a Person sent by Order, they and others aggrieved by any Order of Justices, may appeal to the next Sessions of the County or Place wherein the Parish lies, from whence the poor Person is removed, as I have already intimated; but on the Appeal, the Sessions may order Costs to be paid by the Overseers of the Poor, or other Person against whom 'tis determin'd; and it is the same on giving Notice to a proper Officer to appeal, and not prosecuting the Appeal. The Costs may be levied by Distress and Sale of the Goods of the Person order'd to pay it, by a Justice's Warrant; and if no Distress can be had, the Party shall be committed to Gaol for twenty Days. *8 & 9 W.3. c.30.*

    Church-wardens and Overseers, for every Neglect and Default in executing their Offices relating to the Poor, forfeit the Sum of 20s. to be employed to the Use of the Poor of the Parish: The Default to be proved either by Confession or Oath of one Witness, and the Penalty levied by the new Church-wardens and Overseers, by Distress and Sale, by Virtue of a Warrant from one Justice; and for want of Distress, two Justices may commit the Offender 'till Payment. *43 Eliz. c.2.; Dalt.97.*

The Act 5 Geo.1. c.8. concerning Families left on Parishes.

    The Church-wardens or Overseers of the Poor, where any Wife, Child or Children, shall be left on the Charge of any Parish, making Application to and by Warrant from two Justices of Peace, may seise so much of the Goods and Chattels, and receive so much of the Rents and Profits of the Lands and Tenements of the

Husband, Father, *etc.* of such Wife or Children, as the Justices shall direct, for the Discharge of the Parish, in providing for such Wife or Children.

And at the next Quarter-Sessions, the Warrant of the two Justices being confirm'd, the Justices in their Sessions may make an Order for the Church-wardens or Overseers, to dispose of the Goods or Chattels by Sale thereof; and also to receive the said Rents and Profits of the Lands and Tenements, or so much of them as they shall think fit.

And the Church-wardens, *etc.* are to be accountable for all Money as they receive, to the Justices in Sessions.

The new Act 9 Geo.1. c.7. for providing Houses, etc. for the Poor.

Justices of Peace are not to order Relief to poor Persons, until Oath be made of reasonable Cause; and that they had applied to the Parishioners at some Vestry or publick Meeting, or to the Overseers of the Poor of the Parish, and were refused to be relieved by them; and until the Justices hath summoned the Overseers to shew Cause why Relief should not be given. All Persons order'd by Justices to be relieved, must be Registered in the Parish-Books, as those who are to receive Collection; and no Officer of any Parish shall bring to the Parish Account, any Money he shall give to poor Persons not registered in the Parish-Books, on Pain of £5 Penalty, leviable by Distress, by Warrant of two Justices, for the Use of the Poor of the Parish. But there is an Exception in the Act, as to relieving Persons upon emergent Occasions.

Church-wardens and Overseers of the Poor, with the Consent of the major Part of the Parishioners, have Power by this Statute to purchase or hire any House or Houses in the Parish or Place, and contract with Persons for Lodging, Keeping and Employing of poor Persons; and there they are to keep them, and take the Benefit of their Work and Labour, for the better Maintenance and Relief of such Persons: And poor Persons refusing to be so lodg'd, kept and maintained, are to be struck out of the Parish-Books, and not be intitled to Relief. Two or more Parishes, where small, with the Approbation of a Justice of Peace, may unite in purchasing or hiring Houses for the aforesaid Purposes: And the Church-wardens and Overseers of the Poor of one Parish, with the Consent of the Majority of the Parishioners, may contract with the Church-wardens, *etc.* of any other Parish, for the Lodging and Maintenance of Poor. And no Persons, or their Apprentices, Children, *etc.* shall acquire a Settlement in the Parish, to which they shall be remov'd.

No Person shall gain a Settlement in any Parish, by Virtue of any Purchase therein, for which the Consideration doth not amount *bona fide* to £30 for any longer Time than such Person shall inhabit in the Estate purchased; and shall after be liable to Removal to the Place where last legally settled. Persons taxed to the Highways, or on the Scavenger's Rates, shall not acquire any legal Settlement thereby in any Town or Parish where paid.

In Case of Appeals from Orders for Removal of Poor; none shall be proceeded upon in the Quarter-Sessions, unless reasonable Notice be given by the Church-wardens or Overseers of the Poor of the Parish making the Appeal to the Church-wardens, *etc.* of the Parish from which such poor Person shall be removed. If reasonable Time of Notice be not given, the Justices may adjourn the Appeal to the next Quarter-Sessions; and if the Justices in their Sessions, determine in Favour of the Appellant, they are to award so much Money as shall be reasonably expended by the Parish, on whose Behalf the Appeal was made, for the Relief of the poor Person, between the Time of the undue Removal and the Determination of the Appeal.

And this shall be recover'd in like Manner, as Costs upon an Appeal.

A Contract for Lodging and Maintaining poor Persons.

It is contracted and agreed this Day and Year, *etc.* between *A.B.* and *C.D.* Church-wardens, and *E.F.* and *G.H.* Overseers of the Poor of the Parish of, *etc.* in the County of, *etc.* and *J.K.* of, *etc.* that he the said *J.K.* shall and will, during the Term of, *etc.* next coming, at his own proper Costs and Charges, in the House of, *etc.* hired by the said *A.B.* and *C.D. etc.* find, provide and allow, or cause to be found, provided and allowed unto and for *T.W.; R.T.; L.J. etc.* poor Persons of the Parish of, *etc.* aforesaid, sufficient Lodging, Meat, Drink, and all other Necessaries for their and every of their Keeping and Maintenance; he the said *J.K.* being paid and allowed by them the said *A.B.; C.D.; E.F. etc.* the Church-wardens and Overseers of, *etc.* aforesaid, the Weekly Sum of, *etc.* for the same, which they the said *A.B.; C.D.* and *E.F. etc.* do hereby covenant for themselves and their Successors, well and truly to pay, or cause to be paid to the said *J.K.* as the same shall become due; or he the said *J.K.* being allowed the Work, Labour, and Service of them the said *T.W.; R.J.; L.J. etc.* from Time to Time, in such Work and Labour as he the said *J.K.* shall think fit to employ them about; which the said *A.B.* and *C.D. etc.* the Church-wardens and Overseers of the Poor aforesaid, do consent and agree he shall have accordingly. *Witness, etc.*

The New Act 3 Geo.2. c.29. relating to Certificates.

The Witnesses to Certificates of Church-wardens and Overseers of the Poor, acknowledging any poor Person to be legally settled in their Parish, are to make Oath before the Justices of Peace directed to allow the same, that they did see the Persons, whose Names and Seals are thereto, sign and seal the said Certificates; and the Justices shall certify that such Oath was made before them, and thereupon the Certificates shall be allowed as Evidence in all Courts, without further Proof, *etc.*

And when Overseers of the Poor of any Parish remove back any Certificate Persons becoming chargeable to the Parish to which they belong, they shall be reimbursed the Charges in maintaining and removing such Persons, being ascertained by a Justice of Peace, by the Church-wardens or Overseers of the Poor of the Parish to which remov'd.

On default of Payment whereof, the same to be levied by Distress and Sale of their Goods, by Virtue of the Justices Warrant, *etc.*

The New Act *6 Geo.2. c.31.* for Relief of Parishes against Bastard Children.

See Bastards.

Work-houses for the Poor, erected by Statute in particular Places.

The most considerable Work-house in the City of *London*, is that in *Bishopsgate-Street*, set up pursuant to the *13 & 14 Car.2.* By which Act Power is granted for the President and Governors of this Corporation, to purchase or take any

Lands or Tenements not exceeding £3000 *per Ann.* and any Goods or Chattels, *etc.*

In this Work-house, some Hundreds of idle Persons are constantly employ'd in beating of Hemp, picking Oakum, *etc.* And as some are discharg'd, others are committed: But the greatest Benefit arises from the poor Children there maintained; who are religiously educated and employed in spinning of Wool, Knitting and Sewing, *etc.* They are dieted and cloathed, and taught to Read, Write and cast Account, whereby they are qualified for Services and Employments.

The President, *etc.* of this Work-house is impowered to apprehend Vagrants, sturdy Beggars, *etc.* and set them to work.

By the Stat. *7 & 8 W.3.* a great Work-house was erected in the City of *Bristol*, for the better employing and maintaining the Poor; governed by a Corporation, consisting of the Mayor and Aldermen, Guardians and Assistants, *etc.* who may raise Money by a Tax on the Inhabitants, for the Maintenance of the Poor in the said Work-house, not exceeding what hath been usually paid; they have Power to hold Courts for regulating the Affairs of the Poor, and make By-Laws for Government; and to provide what Necessaries they think fit for setting the Poor to work; and compel idle People and Beggars to dwell and inhabit in such Work-houses, and work there; also to keep poor Children in order to be placed out Apprentice.

This Corporation hath the Care of and providing for all the Poor of the said City; except such as are relieved by charitable Gifts, Hospitals, Alms-houses, *etc.*

In the Third Year of Queen *Anne* a Law was made for erecting a Corporation to provide for the poor in the City of *Worcester*, and by this Act the Corporation is to consist of the Mayor, Alderman, several of the Common Council, and others chosen out of each Parish, *etc.* which Corporation is empower'd to hold Courts, summon Persons, *etc.* And also to provide Materials for setting the Poor on Work; oblige idle Persons and the Poor receiving Alms to dwell and work in the Work-house, *etc.*

And they have Power to contract with any Parish in the County of *Worcester*, for the relieving, employing, and setting to work of poor Persons.

By *13 Geo.1.* a Corporation is established for the better providing for and setting at work the Poor in the City of *Gloucester*, consisting of thirty-one Guardians, chosen out of the several Wards and Parishes, at Vestries held by the Church-wardens and Overseers of the Poor, *etc.* The Corporation may make By-Laws for better Government of the same, the Revenues thereof, and for the Maintenance of all such Poor as shall be taken into their Care, *etc.* And they are to charge how many weekly or other Payments shall be needful for maintaining the Poor in their Work-houses; by Certificate to the Mayor and Aldermen of the said City, who shall order the same to be raised and levied on the Inhabitants.

Also they may possess themselves of all the Goods and Effects of those who seek to them for Relief, or that are brought into the Work-house.

The *1 Geo.2.* Enacts, that there shall be a Corporation to continue for ever within the City of *Canterbury*, for the Employing and Maintaining the Poor there; it consists of the Mayor, Recorder, and Justices of the said City, and twenty-eight other Persons elected out of the ablest Inhabitants, two out of each Parish: And they are to erect Work-houses, and raise Money by a Rate or Cess on the Inhabitants, *etc.* The Guardians may make Allowance to poor Persons who fall sick, or are ancient, without compelling them to come into the Work-house; and are to cloath and maintain sixteen poor Blue-Coat Boys separate and apart, and cause them to be instructed in Reading, Writing, *etc.* who are to be put out Apprentices, *etc.*

The Corporation is to provide for all the Poor of the fourteen Parishes; and cause the Church-wardens and Overseers to complain to two Justices of Peace of the said City, in order to remove such Poor as are likely to become chargeable to the Place of their Settlement, *etc.*

Of Orders for Removal of Poor by Justices, etc.

As to *Orders for Removal*, an Order for removing a poor Person to a Place which the Order mentions to be, as the Justices are informed, the Place of his last Settlement, is not good, except it says the Information is upon Oath; but if on Appeal, the Order is confirm'd, it is good. *5 Mod. Ca.325.*

An Order for Removal of a poor Person was quash'd because there was no Judgment of the Justices concerning the last legal Settlement; but only the Oath of a Woman, *etc. 2 Salk.485.*

A Settlement by Order of Justices in Sessions upon an Appeal is good and binding; but if it do not appear that the Cause came before the Justices by Way of Appeal, it may be quash'd, for without that they have no Jurisdiction. *Ibid.481.*

If a poor Family, after an Order of Sessions for their Removal on Appeal, return to the Parish from whence they were remov'd, the Sessions must see their Order of Settlement obey'd; though if such poor Family go into another Parish, not concerned in the Appeal, two Justices of the Peace ought by an original Order to remove them to the Parish where they were settled by the Sessions Order. *2 Salk.482, 489.*

The Order of two Justices not appeal'd from, binds the Parish upon which it is made, 'till a new Settlement is gained. An Order reversed is final only between the Parties; but an Order confirm'd, *etc.* is final to all the World. *Ibid.*

On Appeals to Justices in their Sessions, they are to cause Defects in Form, in Orders, to be rectified without Charge, and then determine the Matters, *etc.* And no *Certiorari* shall be allowed to remove the same into *B.R.* without entering into Recognizance of £50 to prosecute with Effect, and pay Costs if Judgment affirm'd; and on Refusal, or not performing it, the Justices to confirm their Order. *Stat. 5 Geo.2. c.19.*

An Order to remove a Person to his Place of Settlement.

Whereas it appears to us *W.B.* and *J.S.* Esqs; two of his Majesty's Justices of Peace for the County of, *etc.* (one whereof of the *Quorum*) on the Complaint of *A.B.; C.D.; E.F. etc.* Church-wardens and Overseers of the Poor of the Parish of, *etc.* in the County aforesaid, that *L.J.* being on, *etc.* settled in the Parish of, *etc.* is now come into the said Parish of, *etc.* to endeavour to obtain a Settlement in the said Parish, not having done any Act as the Law requires, to make him a Parishioner there, whereby he is likely to become chargeable to the Parish of, *etc.* aforesaid; *And whereas* it appeareth by the Oath of, *etc.* that the said *L.J.* was last legally settled at the Parish of, *etc.* which we do adjudge accordingly: *Now* we the aforesaid Justices do hereby order the said *L.J.* forthwith to remove and depart out of and from the Parish of, *etc.* to the said Parish of, *etc.* the Place of his last legal Settlement; and that in Default thereof, you the Constable of, *etc.* do convey him the said *L.J.* unto the said Parish of, *etc.* and deliver him to the Church-wardens and Overseers of the Poor there, or some or one of them; hereby also requiring you the said Church-wardens, *etc.* of the said Parish of, *etc.* to receive the said *L.J.* as your lawful Parishioner, and provide for him accordingly. *Given, etc.*

SURVEYORS, *etc.*
Of Surveyors of the Highways and Scavengers, their particular Business, etc.

Before I come to the Office of Surveyors of the Highways, I shall let you know what are Highways, and what are private Ways in the Eye of the Law.

And first, Any Cart, Horse, or Foot-way, common to all People, is the King's Highway; (whether it directly lead to any Market-Town or not) and a Nusance in any of the said Ways, is punishable by Indictment. *6 Mod.255.* And if there be an Highway in an open Field, when the Fields are bad in the Winter, Travellers may go on the Outlets of the Lands adjoining, being warranted by Custom: For the King's Subjects are to have a good Passage, and such Outlets are Parcel of the Way. *1 Roll. Abr.390.; Dalt.98.*

In a Highway the King hath but the free Passage for him and his People; but the Freehold, and all the Profits are to the Lord of the Manor, and he may have an Action for eating the Grass, or for Trees taken away, *etc. Dalt.76.*

A private Way is that which leads from a Village, *etc.* to the Parish Church, or Fields, without any Communication with a great Road; which is to be repaired by the Village or Hamlet, and sometimes by a private Person; (*contra* of Highways, the whole Parish shall be charged). If such a Way be out of Repair, every Inhabitant may bring an Action; and for stopping the Way to the Church, they may have an Action upon the Case. *1 Vent.208.*

All Highways of Common Right are to be repaired by the Inhabitants of the Parish in which the Way lies; unless there be some special Matter to fix the Repairs upon others; as where a Person by an Enclosure streightens a Highway on both Sides, though the Parish repaired it before, yet now he is obliged to maintain it at his own Charge; but if he lays open the Enclosure, so that the Wat remains as it did before, then the Parish is to repair it again. *Cro. Car.366.*

Term. Pasb. 7 Jac.1. It was resolv'd, That all the Country ought to repair a Highway, where no particular Persons are bound to repair, because the whole Country have their Ease and Passage by it. *Co. Rep.13.*

A Person may be obliged to repair a Way by Tenure of Lands; and Lands have been often given for the Maintenance of Highways. See Statute *22 Car.2.* A particular Person may be bound to repair a Highway by Prescription; and so may a Corporation. *Latch. Rep.206.*

The King by the Common Law might award his Commission for amending the Highways and Bridges throughout the Realm. *Dalt.77.* And no Highway can be changed, *etc.* Without the King's Writ of *Ad quod damnum,* and Licence thereupon, on Enquiry whether it will be prejudicial to the Publick, *etc. 3 Cro.267.*

But the Statutes ordain, that for the Repairs of Highways, Surveyors shall be yearly chosen in every Parish, by Constables, Church-wardens, *etc.* and the Inhabitants thereof, as appears by *2 & 3 P.& M. c.8.* And by the Statute *3 & 4 W.& M. c.12.* Surveyors of the Highways are to be chosen in the following Manner.

On the 26th of *December* yearly, the Parishioners are to assemble together, and make a List of a competent Number of Persons qualified to serve the Office, *viz.* such as have an Estate of £10 *per Annum,* either in their own Right, or in Right of their Wives, or who rent £30 *per Annum,* or are worth £100 in personal Estate: And for want of such, a List must be made of the most substantial Persons.

This List is to be return'd by the Constables, or two or more Justices of the Peace, at a special Sessions, held the Third of *January* following, or within Fifteen Days afterwards: Out of which the Justices in their Sessions, are to appoint one or more to be Surveyors, *etc.* by an Order under their Hands and Seals.

And a Person appointed Surveyor by the Justices, not taking upon him the Offfice, having Notice given by the Constables in six Days, and being served with the Order of the Justices, he is liable to the Penalty of £5 one Moiety to the Informer, and the other to be applied in the Reparation of the Highways. *Stat. 3 & 4 W.& M.*

Upon the Refusal of the Party nominated by the Justices in their Sessions to be Surveyor, and paying the Forfeiture of £5 (which is to be levied by Warrant from the said Justices, granted upon Oath made of such Refusal by one Witness) the Justices are to appoint some other fit Person, who upon Notice is to take upon him the Office, under the like Penalty.

The Justices shall hold a special Sessions in their Divisions, every Year on the Third of *January*, or within Fifteen Days after; of which they are to give ten Days Notice to all Constables. And they are also to hold a Sessions for the Highways every four Months, under the Penalty of £5. *Stat. 1 Geo.1. c.52.*

At this Sessions the Justices may order the Reparation of those great Roads which most want repairing in the Hundred where the Sessions is held; which shall be first repaired, and in what Time and Manner. *Stat. Ibid.*

Surveyors of the Highways are within Fourteen Days after the Acceptance of their Office, and so from Time to Time every four Months, to view the Roads, *etc.* and to present upon Oath, at the special Sessions, such Ways as are not in Repair, or they forfeit £5 unless two Justices shall allow their Excuse. *Stat. 1 Geo.1.*

A Presentment of a Highway out of Repair.

I *A.B.* Surveyor of the Highways of and within the Parish of, *etc.* in the County of, *etc.* do hereby present, that the Highway leading from, *etc.* to, *etc.* in the said Parish, is very much out of Repair, and dangerous to all Travellers who pass that Road, and that the Inhabitants of the said Parish of, *etc.* ought to repair and amend the same. *A.B.*

They are to give publick Notice from Time to Time every Four Months, in the Parish Church, the next *Sunday* after Sermon ended, of what Defaults they find in the Reparation of the Ways; and if they are not amended by those who ought to do it in thirty Days, then the Surveyors must, within other thirty Days next following, repair the same, and shall be paid the Charges by the Party who should have done the same.

In Case, when Notice is given as aforesaid, the Party do not repair the Ways in the Time limited; and if the Surveyors do amend them, and the Party neglecting, refuseth to pay the Charges, then upon Oath made of Notice, *etc.* as aforesaid, the Surveyor shall be repaid such Expences as a Justice shall think fit, to be levied by his Warrant. *Stat. 3 & 4 W.& M.*

Surveyors not giving an Account of the Defects of Highways, and of those who are bound to find Labourers and Teams, forfeit £5 except the Justices in their Special Sessions allow a reasonable Excuse. *Stat. 1 Geo.1. c.52.*

They are to take the first seasonable Time, to repair the Ways before Harvest; and to appoint six Days for providing Materials, Carriages, *etc.* giving Notice of the Days appointed, at which Time, all Persons liable must Work, and the Ways are to be amended before the Feast of St. *Luke.*

Justices of Peace must particularly express what Days are appointed for working on the Highways; and not fix Days generally between such a Time and such a Time, which will be naught in an Indictment. *Pasch. 2 Ann. B.R.*

Every Person in the Parish occupying a Plough-Land in Tillage or Pasture, and every other Person keeping a Draught or Plough, shall send out a Wain or Cart, furnished with Oxen, Horses, or other Cattle, and two able Men, every Day appointed by the Surveyor, upon Pain of 10s. for every Default. *Stat. 2 & 3 P.& M. c.8; 22 Car.2. c.12.*

If all the Carriages in the Parish shall not be thought necessary by the Surveyors, then the Person whose Carriage is spared is to send out two able Men to labour the Days appointed, or shall forfeit 1s. a Day for every Man not sent. *Ibid.*

Every Housholder, Cottager and Labourer, being no hired Servant, must either work himself for Repairs of the Highways, or hire a sufficient Labourer to work each of the six Days, on Pain of forfeiting 1s. 6d. *per* Day. *22 Car.2.*

And by an ancient Statute, Cottagers assessed at 40s. a Year in Lands, or five Pounds in Goods, to the Payment of any Subsidy to the Crown, not chargeable to the Highways, but as Cottagers, are to find two able Men. *Stat. 18 Eliz. c.10.*

Persons and Carriages are to be provided with Shovels, Spades, Pick-Axes, and other Tools and Instruments necessary; and shall work eight Hours in the Day. *Stat. 22 Car.2.*

In Places where Carts are not used, the Inhabitants shall send Horses, according to the Custom of the Place, with able Persons under the like Penalties.

If any Man hath a Plough-Land in several Parishes, he shall be chargeable only in the Parish where he lives; but if he keep several Plough-Lands in several Parishes, he shall be chargeable in every Parish. *18 Eliz. cap.10.*

A Plough-Land was formerly an Hundred Acres; since Eighty Acres of Land. And by *Stat. 7 & 8 W.3. c.29.* £50 *per Ann.* is declared a Plough-Land.

He who keeps a Draught, and but two Horses, ought to attend therewith for Reparation of the Highways. *Dalt.105.*

A Man keeps a Cart for Hire, and goes with one or two Horses, he must send his Cart to the Amendment of the Highways, with as many Horses as he goes withal. And Brewers, Bricklayers, *etc.* in *Middlesex,* have been adjudg'd to send so many Draughts as they keep. *Mich. 27 Car.2.*

A Person keeping a Coach and Pair of Horses, is bound to send out a Wain towards the Repairs of Highways; a Coach and Horses doing equal Damage to the Ways, as a Cart and Horses. *1 Lev.139.*

If a Man keeps Draughts in a Parish, he is obliged to send a Team for each Draught, whether he occupy any Land in the Parish or not; and he who occupies several Plough-Lands, ought in like Manner to send Teams for each, whether he keep any Draught or not. *Raym.185; 3 Keb.567.*

If the Owner of Lands neither occupy nor let them, but suffer them to lie fresh, he shall be charged as much as if he had occupied them. *Palm.389.*

Upon Default of sending Carriages, and working on the Highways, *etc.* the Surveyors are to complain to the next Justice of Peace, who upon Oath made of the Default, will issue out his Warrant, to levy the Forfeitures by Distress and Sale, *etc.* to be employed towards Amending of the Ways.

It is no Excuse for the Inhabitants of a Parish indicted at Common Law, for not Repairing the Highways, that they have done the Work required by Statute; for the Statutes are in Aid of the Common Law: And when the Statute Work is not sufficient, Rates and Assessments are to be made. *Dalt. c.26.*

And where Defendants have made a Highway as good as it is capable of being made, it is said this shall not discharge them, on an Information; tho' it may be a Mitigation of their Fine. *3 Salk.183.*

But the Defendants are not bound to put the Highway in better Repair than it has been Time out of Mind. *1 Salk.358.*

Where the Statute-Work falls short in repairing of Highways, the Justices in their Quarter-Sessions, being satisfied thereof, may cause Assessments to be made on every Person usually rateable to the Poor, not exceeding 6d. in the Pound of the yearly Value of Lands, *etc.* which Assessments not being paid in Ten Days after Demand, may be levied by Distress. *Stat. 3 & 4 W.& M. c.12.* And notwithstanding the six Days Work have not been performed, these Rates may be made, and the Money disposed of: But the raising Money by Assessment, shall not excuse the Work of any Teams or Labourers by Law appointed to work on the Ways. *Stat. 1 Geo.1. c.52.*

And when Surveyors have laid out their Money on Materials, as Stone, Sand, *etc.* in Parishes where they have none, for Repairing of the Highways, on their making Oath before the Justices at their Special Sessions, of what they have expended, two Justices in the said Sessions, may by Warrant under their Hands and Seals, cause a Rate to be made, for reimbursing the Surveyors, upon every Inhabitant, Parson, Vicar, and other Occupier of Lands, Tithes, Woods, *etc.* in the Parish; which Rate being allowed by the said Justices in their Special Sessions, may be levied on Persons refusing to pay the same, by Distress and Sale, *etc. Stat. 3 & 4 W.& M.*

And two Justices of Peace, in their Special Sessions, may cause a Rate to be made for reimbursing a Person, where a Fine or Penalty is levied on him, for the Parish's Neglect in Repairing of the Highways.

Persons aggrieved by Assessments, may appeal to the Quarter-Sessions, whose

Order shall be final.

Form of an Assessment for Repairing of Highways.

An Assessment made on the Inhabitants of the Parish of, *etc.* in the County of, *etc.* for the Repairing and Amending of the Highways in the said Parish, the Year, *etc.*

	£	s	d
A.B. Esq;	0	7	0
C.D. Gent.	0	5	0
E.F. Yeoman	*0*	*5*	*0*
G.H. etc.	*0*	*6*	*0*
J.K. etc.	*0*	*4*	*0*

Memorandum, This Day and Year, *etc.* the above Assessment was allowed and confirmed by us *L.M.* and *J.S.* Esqs., two of his Majesty's Justices of Peace for the County of, *etc.* aforesaid: And we do hereby impower *L.D.* Surveyor of the Highways in the said Parish, to ask, demand and levy the same of the several Persons above-mentioned, as the Act of Parliament directs; and if not paid in Ten Days, to levy the same by Distress and Sale of their Goods. *Given, etc. L.M. J.S.*

These are the Methods of Taxation for the Highways; and the Statute *7 & 8 W. c.29.* enacts, That if the 6d. in the Pound order'd by *3 & 4 W.& M.* be not sufficient to repair the Ways, after the same is levied and employed, the Justices in their Special Sessions held every four Months, may order the whole Parish to make good the Repairs thereof.

Surveyors of the Highways may take Rubbish ready digged in or near any Quarry, for Repairing of the Ways, without Leave of the Owner; and gather Stones in any Land, without being Trespassers: But they cannot dig for Stones without the Consent of the Owner of the Land. *5 Eliz. c.13.*

But notwithstanding Surveyors may not dig for Stones, they may dig Gravel in any Ground contiguous to the Highway; except it be in a Garden, Orchard, Meadow, *etc.* provided it be but in one Pit or Hole, not above ten Yards over at most; and that the Hole be filled with Earth at the Charge of the Parish within a Month: Not filling up the Pit to forfeit five Marks. *Ibid.*

Surveyors have Authority to turn a Watercourse or Spring of Water out of a Highway into any Ditch of the Ground adjacent; to make Sluices to such Ditches; and to make new Ditches and Drains in and through the Land, next adjoining, where the old Ditches, *etc.* are not sufficient to cary off the Water, and to come upon any of the said Lands with Workmen for that Purpose, and to keep them scoured, *etc. Stat. 5 Eliz.*

A Surveyor is to make every Cart-way leading to a Market-Town, eight Feet broad at least, and, as near as may be, level; and Causeways for Horses, must be three Feet broad. *Stat. 3 & 4 W.& M. c.12.*

And Justices of Peace in their Quarter-Sessions, or five of them, have Power to enlarge or widen any Highways, in their respective Counties, Ridings, Divisions, *etc.* so that the Ground to be taken into the said Highways do not exceed eight Yards in Breadth; and no House be pulled down, or Ground of any Garden, Orchard, Court or Yard be taken away; and making such Satisfaction for Damages, not exceeding Twenty-five Years Purchase, as a Jury impanelled by the said Justices shall assess. *Stat. 8 & 9 W.3. cap.15.*

The Justices may order the Money to be raised by a Rate and Assessment, not above 6d. in the Pound, as Monies are levied for Repairs of the Highways.

Justices of Peace are to issue their Precepts to the Owners of the Ground, to shew Cause why the Highways should not be enlarged: And the Proprietors of Lands taken into Highways, may cut down Timber, *etc.*

Persons laying any Thing in a Highway, not being Twenty Feet broad, forfeit five Shillings: And if Timber, Hay, Straw, Stubble, or other Matter for making Dung, *etc.* shall be laid in any Highway, those who possess Lands adjoining, may remove and dispose thereof to their own Use. *Stat. 3 & 4 W.& M.*

Logs of Timber are not to be laid in any Highway, tho' there be sufficient Room for Travellers left. And no Trees, Shrubs or Bushes shall grow or stand in, or Bough or Branch overhang a Highway, under the Penalty of five Shillings. They are to be cut down by the Owners of the Soil within Ten Days after Notice given by the Surveyors, under the like Penalty, to be levied by Distress; one Moiety to go to the Informer, the other towards the Repairing of the Ways. *3 & 4 W.& M. c.12.*

Injuries to Highways, as laying Logs of Timber, erecting Gates therein, or making Hedges overthwart them; digging Ditches, or suffering Ditches adjoining to the Highways to be foul, which render the Way less commodious to the King's People, are publick Nusances at Common Law, and also by the Statutes. *Kitch. 34, 35.; 8 H.7.; 2 Rol. Abr.137.*

The Soil of Highways belongs to him whose Land it is on each Side. And in whosoever's Ground or Side a Hedge shall be, to the Owner of that Land belongs the keeping of the same Hedge, and the Ditch adjoining and belonging to it on the other Side, in Repair and scoured. *2 Leon.148.*

Those who have Lands adjoining to the Highway, by the Statute *5 Eliz.* must scour their Ditches, as often as there is Occasion, and lay Trunks or Bridges over them where there are Cart-ways in a Ground, that the Water may have a free Passage, under the Penalty of 1s. *per* Rod.

By the Statute *3 & 4 W.& M.* if they neglect to do it in ten Days after Notice, the Forfeiture is five Shillings. And by the Statute *1 Geo.1. cap.52.* Persons who delay to scour and keep open Ditches near the Highways, 30 Days after Notice given by the Surveyors to do it, on Oath thereof made before the Justices at their Special Sessions, forfeit 2s. 6d. for every 8 Yards of Ditching not scoured, *etc.* to be levied by Distress and Sale, *etc.*

If in scouring Ditches any Person shall lay the Soil in the Highway, and not carry it away within 10 Days after Notice, he shall be liable to a Penalty of one Shilling *per* Load. *Stat. 3 & 4 W.& M.* But if it be not removed in eight Days after Notice, he forfeits not exceeding five Pounds, nor under twenty Shillings, by *1 Geo.1.*

Those Persons who pull up, cut or remove any Post, Block or Stone, or other Security set up for securing Foot Causeways, *etc.* from Waggons and Carts, shall forfeit 20s. for every Offence. *Stat. 7 & 8 W.3. cap.29.*

Surveyors of the Highways neglecting to erect or fix a Stone or Post, where two or more cross Highways meet, with an Inscription thereon in large Characters, as a Direction for Travellers, containing the Name of the next Market-Town, to which each of the adjoining Highways leads, according to a Precept from Justices of Peace at their Sessions, shall forfeit 10s. *Stat. 8 & 9 W.3. c.16.*

No travelling Waggon wherein any Burdens shall be carried, (except of Manure for Lands and Husbandry, Hay, Straw, Corn unthreshed, Coal, Timber, and Materials for Building, Stone, Artillery, *etc.*) shall be drawn in Highways, with more than six Horses, Oxen or Beasts, under the Penalty of five Pounds, one Moiety to the Prosecutor, the other for Repairs of the Ways.

The Penalty is to be levied by Distress of the Horses or Oxen of the Owner of the Waggon in three Days, by Virtue of a Justice's Warrant: And any Person may distrain or seize Horses, *etc.* and deliver them to the Surveyor or other Parish-Officer. *Stat. 9 Ann. cap.18.*

The Person seizing, *etc.* neglecting to bring the Cattle to the Surveyor, forfeits Twenty Pounds: And the Surveyor neglecting to deliver the Sum by him received to the Justice, is liable to the same Penalty, to be levied by Distress.

Persons imployed by Carriers or others, and driving or assisting in the Driving any travelling Waggon with more than six Horses, *etc.* shall be liable to the Penalty of five Pounds, *ut supra:* But where six Horses, *etc.* are not sufficient to draw up Hill, or in foul Way, any Person may, by the Consent of the Owner or Driver, *etc.* add more Horses from any other Cart or Waggon on the Road in the same Highway.

By the Statute *1 Geo.1. c.10.* The Drawing of Waggons and Carts was to be with five Horses, *etc.* in Length, and no more; under the Penalties in the Act *6 Anne.* And this last Act is according to the first Statute made on this Head, in the 22d and 23d Years of King *Charles* II.

But by *5 Geo.1. cap.12.* travelling Waggons are to be drawn with six Horses; and Carts with three. Travelling with more, the extraordinary Horses shall be forfeited to the Seizor: And travelling Waggons must have their Wheels bound with Iron two Inches and an Half broad, or be liable to forfeit all the Horse above three in Number: And hindering the Seizure incurs a Forfeiture of £10.

Surveyors shall give an Account upon Oath, at a Special Sessions, of all Monies that come to their Hands, and how disposed, *etc.* And if any remains, they are to deliver it over to the next Surveyors, or forfeit double the Value of what shall be in their Hands.

Justices in their Special Sessions may examine on Oath, any Person who can give an Account of Money, which ought to be applied for mending the Highways; and levy the Penalties, *etc.* And the next Quarter-Sessions may make such Order as they think fit, where any Person shall find himself aggriev'd. *Stat. 1 Geo.1. c.52.*

Stewards of Leets have Power to inquire into the Breach of the Stat. *2 & 3 P.& M.* for Repairing Highways, and to set Fines, *etc. 2 & 3 P.& M. c.8.*

Any Justice may upon his own Knowledge present at the Quarter-Sessions any

87

Offence concerning the Highways, upon which the Court may assess a Fine. *Stat. 5 Eliz. c.13.*

Also one Justice upon his own View, *etc.* may commit him who resists any Person imployed to put the Acts in Execution relating to the Highways, or rescuing Goods distrained, unless he pay 40s. to the Surveyor within seven Days. *Stat. 22 Car.2.*

By former Statutes, the Penalty is forty Shillings for Neglects of Surveyors in putting the Laws in Execution for repairing the Highways; but by the Statute *6 Ann. cap.29.* the Forfeiture is made Five Pounds. And by *1 Geo.1.* Surveyors misapplying Money, are liable to the like Penalty of five Pounds.

Justices neglecting or refusing to do what is required by the *Stat. 3 & 4 W.& M.* for amending the Highways, shall forfeit £5. And Justices of Peace of all Cities and Corporations, *etc.* are to put these Acts in Execution.

All Matters concerning Highways are to be determined in the County where they lie; and the Prosecution to be in six Months after the Offences committed; and no Presentment, Indictment or Order shall be removed from the Quarter-Sessions by *Certiorari. Stat. 3 & 4 W.& M.*

In Indictment for not repairing a Highway, it must be laid to be the King's Highway for all the King's Liege People; and set forth from what Place to what Place it leads, *etc. Hill. 9 W.3. B.R.; Style's Rep.356.*

Where Inhabitants of two adjoining Parishes are indicted, the Indictment ought not to be joint, but several: And if it be against Persons in a Hamlet, within a Parish, it will be quashed; because such Hamlet cannot be charged to repair the Highways, except it is by Prescription, but the whole Parish. *Style 157, 163.*

In a Trial concerning Repairs of Highways, those who are chargeable to the Repairs shall not be admitted as Evidence; but a Person in the Parish, no way liable to such Reparations, will be a good Witness. *Term. Hill.; 14 & 15 Car.2.*

Appointment of a Surveyor by Justices of the Peace.

At a Special Sessions held for the Highways on, etc. at the House, etc.

We whose Names are hereto subscribed, being Justices of the Peace in the County of, *etc.* do hereby appoint *A.B.* of, *etc.* (one of the Persons mentioned in a List this Day returned to us by *C.D.* Constable of, *etc.*) Surveyor of the Highways in the Parish of, *etc.* aforesaid, for and during the Space of one whole Year next ensuing the Date hereof, according to the Form of the Statute in that Case made and provided. *Given under our Hands and Seals, etc.* **T.D. J.S.**

A Warrant to levy the Forfeiture for refusing to serve the Office of Surveyor.

Midd.ss Whereas *A.B.* of, *etc.* was at a Special Sessions held on, *etc.* lawfully appointed to serve the Office of Surveyor of the Highways, in and for the Parish, *etc.* aforesaid, for the Year ensuing; and it having been duly proved before us, that the said *A.B.* had Notice thereof within six Days after the same, and that he hath refused to take upon him the said Office, whereby he hath forfeited the Sum of £5 one Moiety to be paid to, *etc.* who hath informed us of the said Offence, and the other Moiety to be applied towards the Repairing of the Highways: *These* are therefore to command you to levy the said Forfeiture of £5 on the Goods and Chattels of the said *A.B.* by Distress and Sale, to be paid and employed as aforesaid;

88

and that you do forthwith return to us or some other Justices, *etc.* the Names of other Persons within your Parish, fit to serve the said Office of Surveyor, that the Business of the Highways may not be neglected. *Given, etc.*

A Warrant against a Surveyor refusing to account.

Whereas it hath been duly proved before us *T.D.* and *J.S.* Esqrs; two of his Majesty's Justices of Peace for the County aforesaid, that *A.B.* of, *etc.* Surveyor of the Highways in and for the said Parish, hath neglected to give an Account upon Oath, at any Special Sessions, of the Money which hath come to his Hands, and which ought to be employed in amending the Highways, and how he hath disposed thereof, so that for such his Neglect he hath forfeited the Sum of 40s. These are therefore to command you to levy the said Forfeiture, *etc.*

There are several Statutes for erecting *Turnpikes* in Ways, giving Authority to Justices of Peace and Trustees, to appoint Special Surveyors of the Highways, to amend the same; and Collectors of Toll 1d. for every Horse, and 6d. for a Coach, *etc.* accounting to the Justices, *etc.* And all Persons chargeable towards the Repairs of the Highways shall remain so notwithstanding. *4 & 5 W.& M.; 7 & 8 W.3., etc.*

Driving Cattle through Grounds to avoid the Toll, incurs a Forfeiture of 10s. And Offenders cutting down Turnpikes or Gates, shall be committed to the House of Correction for three Months; and a second Offence is made Felony and Transportation. *Stat. 8 Geo.1. c.5.; 1 Geo.2. c.23.*

Persons maliciously breaking down, or plucking up any Turnpike, Gate, *etc.* in a Highway, convicted on Indictment before Justices of Gaol-Delivery, shall be guilty of Felony, and be transported for seven Years; and if the Commissioners or Trustees erect Gates where they have no Power, Justices of Peace in Quarter-Sessions may cause them to be removed, by the Sheriff of the County. By *Stat. 5 Geo.2. c.33.*

Of Scavengers.

The Statutes concerning Scavengers are the *2 W.& M.; 8 & 9 W.3. & 1 Geo.1.* but the first is the most Particular.

By this Statute, two Tradesmen are to be chosen Scavengers yearly in every Parish within the Weekly Bills of Mortality, by the Constables, Church-wardens, *etc.* and other Inhabitants; who must take upon them the Office in seven Days after Election and Notice, under the Penalty of ten Pounds, to be levied by Distress, by Virtue of a Warrant from one Justice; and for want of a Distress, the Offender is to be committed: The Penalty is to be employed in repairing the Highways and Streets in the same Parish. *2 W.& M. Sess.2. c.8.*

Scavengers every Day, except *Sundays* or Holidays, are to bring their Carts into the Streets, and give Notice by a Bell, or otherwise, of carrying away Dirt, and to stay a convenient Time, or shall forfeit £2.

The Inhabitants in *London, Westminster, Kensington, Southwark,* and within the Bills of Mortality, are to sweep their Streets every *Wednesday* and *Saturday,* or they forfeit for every Neglect three Shillings and four Pence. This is increased to ten Shillings by *Stat. 8 & 9 W.3. c.37.*

Persons laying Dirt, *etc.* in the Streets before their Houses, are liable to 5s. Penalty; and laying Ashes, Dirt, *etc.* before the Houses and Walls of others, or before Church-Walls, or throwing any noisome Things in the common Sewer,

Highway, or private Vault, forfeit £1.

And hooping or cleansing Vessels in Streets, Lanes, *etc.* mending Coaches, or sawing Timber or Stones, throwing out Dung, Soil, *etc.* likewise incur a Forfeiture of £1.

But Justices in their Petit Sessions may give Scavengers liberty to lodge their Dirt in vacant Places near the Streets, satisfying the Owners for the Damage; and if the Demands of the Owners are unreasonable, the Justices have a Power to moderate the Price.

Inhabitants of Houses are to keep the Streets, Lanes and Allies before their Doors paved, to the Middle of the Highway, or shall forfeit for every Perch or Rod £1 and if not amended 20s. a Week 'till done: Owners of Houses unoccupied, are liable to the like Penalties.

One Justice may certify to the Sessions what new Ways are fit to be paved; and Owners and Inhabitants of Houses new built, not paving or amending the Ground before their Houses, forfeit £2 for every Perch or Rod, and the like *per* Week for delaying. But when paved, they are only subject to the same Penalty as others.

Justices of *Middlesex* may at their Quarter-Sessions make Rates for paving *Kensington, etc.*

The Justices in Sessions may order an Assessment to be made, not exceeding 4d. *per* Pound for Lands, and 8d. for every £20 personal Estate, every Year; and Constables, Church-wardens, *etc.* may make a Tax, being allowed by two Justices, to be collected quarterly, and be levied by Distress and Sale, *etc.* if not paid within 14 Days.

By the Statute *1 Geo.1. c.52.* for repairing of Highways, the Justices of Peace at the Quarter-Sessions may appoint Scavengers, and order the Repairing and Cleansing the Streets in any City or Market-Town; and appoint Persons to make Assessments on all Owners and Occupiers of Lands and Houses equally, not exceeding six Pence *per* Pound *per Annum* to defray the Charge of such Scavengers, which may be collected by such as the Justices think fit, and levied in eight Days by Distress, *etc.*

The Assessments for Scavengers in the Parishes of St. *Anne* and St. *James,* within the City of *Westminster,* shall be rated according to the Custom of the said City, where it is not otherwise provided.

Ancient Streets of *London* are to be maintained according to Custom; and cleansing of Streets, *etc.* must be managed according to the ancient Usage of the City of *London.* The Lord Mayor, or any Alderman may present upon View any Offence within the City and Liberties thereof; and assess Fines not exceeding twenty Shillings for every Offence, to be paid to the Chamberlain for the Use of the City. *Stat. 2 W.& M.*

Scavengers, when new ones are chosen, must account in 28 Days before two Justices of Peace, for the Monies assessed and collected, and what remains in their Hands must be paid to the new Officers; refusing to account, they shall be committed 'till they do, and 'till Payment is made.

The Penalties *supra* are recoverable by Distress, by Warrant from a Justice, *etc.* to the Constable; and if the Offender is convicted by View of the Justice, one Half of them goes to the Poor, and the other to the Repair of the Ways; but if by Evidence, the Penalties are distributed between the Poor and Prosecutor.

The Housholders within the weekly Bills of Mortality, whose Houses adjoin to the Streets, shall hang out Lights from the Time it grows dark 'till 12 a-Clock at Night, from *Michaelmas* to *Lady-day*, or pay for Lamps, under the Penalty of two Shillings for every Default, *etc.*

Swine may not be kept in Houses or Backsides of the paved Streets, on Pain of Forfeiting them: And Officers may by Warrant from the Lord Mayor, or one Justice, *etc.* search for Swine, and drive away and sell them, and deliver the Money to Church-wardens, *etc.* for the Use of the Poor.

In the Case of the Parish of *Newington*, on the Stat. *2 W.& M.* for paving and cleaning the Streets; the Question was, if Persons that lived out of the Paving, should contribute to the Scavengers Rates; and the Court held the Rate which charged all the Inhabitants generally to be good. *Skin. Rep. 643.*

Persons who are bound to repair the Pavements before their Houses at their own Costs, are also obliged to pay to the Scavengers Tax; for as to paving before their own Doors, they have the principal Benefit of it. *5 Mod. 68.; 1 Salk. 356.*

By the Stat. *8 & 9 W.3. c.17.* Owners of Hay brought into the Hay-Market, are to pay three Pence *per* Load, and for Straw one Penny, to such as Justices of Peace shall appoint, towards mending the Street called the *Hay-Market:* And no Persons shall suffer their Waggons, Carts, *etc.* to stand in any Place within the Weekly Bills of Mortality, loaden with Hay or Straw, from *Michaelmas* to *Lady-day*, after two a-Clock in the Afternoon; nor from *Lady-day* to *Michaelmas*, after three a-Clock, on pain of 5s. for each Offence.

The Wheels of Carts, (Country Carts, those used for carrying Goods Half a Mile beyond the paved Streets, and of Scavengers excepted) are not to be less than six Inches in the Felly, and to be without Iron; and drawn only by two Horses, after they are up the Hills near the Water, under the Penalty of two Pounds for every Cart otherwise. *2 W.& M.*

Any Carman, *etc.* riding in a Cart or Dray, not having another on Foot to guide it, forfeits ten Shillings to the Informer, and the Poor of the Parish. *Stat. 1 Geo.1. cap.57.* And Carts in *London* are not to carry beyond the Quantities of Bricks, Coals, *etc.* appointed, on Pain of forfeiting one of the Horses, *etc. Vide 6 Geo.1. c.6.*

Surveyors of Streets in Westminster by Statute.

The Statute *2 Geo.2. c.11.* ordains, That on the 26th of *December* in every Year, the Constables, Church-wardens and Inhabitants of Parishes in *Westminster, etc.* shall meet together and make a List of the Names of Persons fit to be Surveyors of the Streets, and return them to the Justices at a Special Sessions held in ten Days after; and they are to appoint two or more to the Office under their Hands and Seals.

If the Persons appointed refuse to act, they shall forfeit £20 and the Justices are to nominate other fit Persons to perform the Office, on like Forfeiture on Refusal; and so upon the Death of any Person, *etc.* and if the Constables, *etc.* do not return to the Justices such Lists, they shall forfeit £10.

The Surveyors every six Weeks, or oftner if necessary, are to take a View of all the Streets, Lanes, and Allies in the Places for which appointed; and shall make a

Return on Oath to the Justices at a Special Sessions, to be holden in the Week preceding the Quarter-Sessions, of the Names of Persons whose Pavements are out of Repair; and the Justices are to present the same at the Quarter-Sessions, which is to proceed thereupon.

Publick Notice shall be given in the Church on the next Lord's Day, of all Defaults, *etc.* and if they are not amended in Twenty Days after, the Surveyors may cause them to be repaired, and shall be reimbursed by the Parties who should have done the same; on Oath made of the Charges before a Justice, *etc.*

If any Paving belonging to a House which is empty, shall be out of Repair, the Surveyors are to make it good, and may have it new paved, if the Justices think fit; and the Charges shall be levied on the next Tenant by Distress: And the new Tenant may retain the Sum taken out of his Rent.

And where any Dwelling house, *etc.* is burnt or pull'd down before the Sums are paid, the Money shall be levied in like Manner on any Tenant of the new House erected in the Place of such Building.

Surveyors of the Streets neglecting their Duty, shall forfeit 40s. and the Justices of Peace omitting to do what is required of them, are liable to a Penalty of £5.

By this Act the Justices may order the Amendment of Water pipes and Pavements, where they are irregular or bad. And the Surveyors, or other Persons amending them, shall be repaid by the Proprietors of such Water-works.

And Justices of Peace at any Special Sessions, may give a Reward or Allowance to the Surveyors for their Trouble and Loss of Time, not exceeding £8 *per Annum*, to be paid out of the Scavengers Rates.

This Statute shall not extend to the Royal Palaces, or to St. *James's Square*: And all Laws in Force for cleaning the Streets, Lanes, *etc.* within the Bills of Mortality, are to be duly observ'd, and put in Execution so far as they are consistent with this Act.

And Scavengers and Rakers shall sweep up and lay in Heaps, all the Dirt which they are to carry away, on Forfeiture of 40s.

St. James's Square, *and how Repaired.*

The Statute of *12 Geo.1. c.25.* appoints Commissioners and Trustees, to clean and repair St. *James's Square*, and continue the same cleaned; who may employ Workmen, Labourers and Carters, *etc.* for that Purpose.

Rates to be made and assessed on Houses, at so much *per* Foot in Front, not exceeding 10s. a Year, leviable by Distress, *etc.* The Trustees, by Writing under their Hands, shall appoint a Collector and Receiver of the Rates, and they are to account on Oath, before Justices of Peace, *etc.* and if they refuse to pay the Money to such Persons as the Trustees order, the Justices of *Westminster*, at a Special Sessions, may commit them to Gaol 'till paid.

Three or more of the Trustees may direct the Collector, with Assistance of a Constable, to enter Houses in the Day-Time, and distrain Goods of Persons refusing to pay the Rates, and sell the Distress in five Days, if not replevied; or if a Distress be not proper, the Trustees may bring Action at Law for Money payable.

Persons annoying the Square with Filth, being convicted before one Justice of Peace, incur 20s. Penalty; to be levied by Virtue of the Justice's Warrant; and

The Compleat Parish Officer - Surveyors..

making any Incroachment on the Square, shall forfeit £50.

The *East, West* and *North* Parts of this Square, *etc.* shall be a distinct Ward, as to Scavengers Rates only, and be exempted from paying any other Rates.

The Statutes relating to Hackney-Coaches and Chairs.

By the Statute *9 Ann. c.23.* eight hundred Hackney-Coaches, and two hundred Chairs, are allowed in *London* and *Westminster*, and the Chairs are made up four hundred, by subsequent Statutes.

These Coaches and Chairs are to be licensed by Commissioners; and upon every Licence shall be reserved 5s. *per* Week, payable monthly for each Coach, and 10s. *per Ann.* to be paid quarterly for every Chair. Commissioners licensing above the Number, to forfeit £100.

Persons driving a Hackney-Coach without Licence, shall forfeit £5 and a Chair 40s. And a Person driving a Coach, or carrying a Chair for Hire, not being interested himself in a Licence; or Guilty of any Misdemeanor by giving abusive Language, demanding more than his Fare, *etc.* one Justice may order him to pay, not exceeding 20s. to the Poor; and not being able to pay it, may send him to the House of Correction for seven Days.

Coachmen refusing to go at, or exacting more for Hire, than by the Act is limited, forfeit a Sum not exceeding £3 nor under 10s. at the Discretion of the Commissioners, three or more whereof are to determine the same. By *1 Geo.1. c.57.*

And the Commissioners may make By-Laws, for regulating Hackney-Coachmen, *etc.* And the Rents or Sums reserved, and all Forfeitures and Penalties shall be levied by Warrant of three Commissioners, by Distress and Sale of Goods in Ten Days.

Persons not paying Coachmen their due Fare, or cutting or defacing Coaches, Chairs, *etc.* a Justice shall order them to make Satisfaction; and on Refusal, may bind them over to the Quarter-Sessions.

The Fare of Hackney-Coachmen in *London*, or within ten Miles, is 10s. *per* Day, allowing twelve Hours to the Day; and by the Hour not above 1s. 6d. for the first, and 1s. for every Hour after: And none are obliged to pay above 1s. for the Use of any Hackney-Coach for any Distance (not mentioned in the Act) which is not above one Mile and four Furlongs; nor above 1s. 6d. for any Distance not exceeding two Miles.

The Places and Sums specified by the Act, are 1s. from any of the *Inns* of *Court* to any Part of St. *James's* or *Westminster*, (except beyond *Tothill Street*) and from the said *Inns*, or thereabouts, to the *Royal Exchange*, 1s. and to the *Tower* or *Bishopsgate*, or *Aldgate*, 1s. 6d. and so from the said Places to the said *Inns*: And the like Rates from and to any Places at the like Distance.

In Pursuance of this Act, the Commissioners have caused to be measured and rated several Distances between the most noted Parts of the Town, as follows:

The Rates of Hackney-Coaches for particular Distances, (not specified in the Act) ordered by the Commissioners within the weekly Bills of Mortality.

One Shilling Rates for Coaches.

From *Westminster-Hall* to *Marlborough-Street, Bolton-Street, Soho-Square, Bloomsbury-Square, Little Queen-Street, Holbourn.*

From St. *James's Gate* to *Queen Anne's Square, Westminster*, the nearest Corner of *Red-Lyon-Square.*

From *Golden-Square* to *Red-Lyon-Square.*

From the *Hay-Market* Theatre to *Red-Lyon-Square, Bloomsbury-Square, Queen-Square, Westminster.*

From *Red-Lyon-Square* to *Guild-hall.*

From the upper End of *Fetter-Lane, Holbourn,* to *Aldgate.*

From the *Royal Exchange* to *Hoxton-Square.*

From *Newgate* to the Middle of *Greek-Street,* near *Soho-Square.*

From the *King's Head Tavern, Southwark,* to the Sign of Sir *William Wallworth.*

From *Grays-Inn* to *Sadlers Wells,* by *Islington.*

From *Tom's Coffee-House* in *Russel-Street, Covent-Garden,* to *Newcastle-house* near *Cearkenwell* Church.

From *Temple-Bar* to *Billingsgate.*

From *Aldgate* to *Shadwel* Church.

One Shilling and Six-penny Rates for Coaches.

From *Drury-Lane* Playhouse to *Queen Annes' Square, Westminster.*

From *Westminster-hall* to St. *Paul's* Church or *Queen's Square, Red-Lyon-Fields.*

From St. *James's* Gate to *Hatton Garden.*

From the *New Exchange* in the *Strand* to the *Royal Exchange.*

From the *Hay-Market* Playhouse to *Hatton-Garden.*

From *Westminster-hall* to *Red-Lyon-Square.*

From St. *James's* to *Marybone* Church.

From the *Royal Exchange* to *Bloomsbury-Square,* or to the Watch-house at *Mile-End.*

From the Outside of *Aldgate* to *Stepney* Church.

From *Bedford-Street, Covent Garden,* to *Coleman-Street.*

From *Bread-Street* to *Upper-Moorfields,* and thence to *Hoxton-Square.*

From *Austin Fryars* Gate in *Broad Street* to *Hart-Street* by *Bloomsbury* Market.

From St. *Martin's Lane* in the *Strand* to *Gold-Street* by *Wood-Street.*

From the End of *Lombard Street* next *Gracechurch Street* to *Somerset-house.*

From St. *Lawrence* Church by *Guild-hall,* to *Brownlow-Street* in *Drury-Lane.*

From the *Royal Exchange* to *Newington* Church beyond *Southwark.*

From *Tom's* Coffee-house by *Covent-Garden* to the *Royal Exchange.*

From *Stocks-Market* to *Charing-Cross.*

From *Aldgate* to *Ratcliff Cross.*

The Compleat Parish Officer - The Laws and Statutes.

The Fare of a Hackney-Chair is 1s. for any Distance not exceeding a Mile; and 1s. 6d. for any Distance not exceeding a Mile and four Furlongs: And for particular Distances as follows, viz.

One Shilling Rates for Chairs.

From *Westminster-hall* to *Covent-Garden*, or to *Exeter-Exchange*.

From St. *James's* Gate through the Park to *Westminster-hall*.

From St. *James's* Gate to *Somerset-house*.

From *Somerset-house* to the upper End of *Hatton Garden*.

From the *Hay-Market* Theatre to *Bolton-Street*, *Essex-Street*, *Soho-Square*, Entrance of *Lincoln's Inn-Fields*.

From the nearest Corner of *Golden-Square* to *Drury-Lane* Theatre.

One Shilling and Six-penny Rates for Chairs.

From *Westminster-hall* to *Marlborough-Street*, *Soho-Square*, *Bolton-Street*, *Temple-Bar*.

From St. *James's* Gate to *Queen Anne's Square*, *Westminster*.

From *Golden-Square* to *Red-Lyon-Square*.

From *Red-Lyon-Square* to the *Hay-Market* Play-house.

From *Queen's Square* to the said Play-house.

From the *Hay-Market* Playhouse to *Bloomsbury Square*, or *Grays Inn*.

The most noted Places for standing of Hackney-Coaches, are *Palace-Yard*, *Westminster*, near *Westminster-hall* Gate; near *Scotland-Yard*, *Whitehall*, *Charing-cross*, St. *James's* Palace Gate; *Somerset-house*, *Little Russel-Street*, and *Bedford-Street*, *Covent-Garden*; near St. *Clement's* Church in the *Strand*, *Temple-Bar*, St. *Dunstan's* Church, *Fleet-Street*; near the Gates of the *Inns of Court*, St. *Paul's* Church, *Guild-hall*, *Stocks Market*, the *Royal Exchange*, between *Bishopsgate* and *Devonshire Street* End, *etc.* But by Order of Commissioners, they are to stand in the Middle of the Streets, and not against Gates; or in Streets not 30 Feet wide; nor cross any Street, or within eight Feet of Houses, Walls, *etc.* on Pain of 10s. And the Drivers are to give Way to Persons of Quality, and Gentlemens Coaches, under the like Penalty of 10s.

Hackney-Coachmen not having Tin-plates with the Number of their Coaches, shall forfeit £5. Refusing any Person to take the Number, or giving a wrong Number, to forfeit a Sum not exceeding 40s.

None but licensed Persons shall stand, ply or drive any Coach, Hearse, or Coach-horses for Hire; or shall let to Hire any Mourning-Coach, or Coach-horses, to attend on Funerals, within the weekly Bills of Mortality, under the Penalty of £5. *Stat. 1 Geo.1. cap.57.*

And on *Sundays*, one hundred and seventy-five Coaches only are to Ply, by Persons appointed, under the like Penalty, *etc.*

The Laws and Statutes concerning Watermen.

The Lord Mayor and Court of Aldermen of *London*, are yearly to elect eight of the best Watermen, to be Overseers and Rulers, and keep good Order amongst the Rest; and the Watermen shall chuse Assistants, who may make Rules to be observed under Penalties; and the Lord Mayor and Aldermen, and Justices of Peace are to hear and determine Offences, *etc.* Watermen and Lightermen on the *Thames*, between *Gravesend* and *Windsor*, are made a Company by Statute *2 & 3 P.& M. c.16.; 11 & 12 W.3. c.21.*

Watermen's Names shall be Registered by the Overseers: Their Boats or Wherries must be twelve Foot and a Half long, and four Foot and a Half broad in the Midship, or be liable to Forfeiture; and two Watermen shall not ply, but where one of them hath exercised the Profession two Years, and been allowed by the Overseers. And Watermen taking more than the Rates or Fares appointed, shall forfeit 40s. and suffer Half a Year's Imprisonment; and refusing to carry Persons for their Fare, be imprison'd twelve Months. *Ibid.*

Forty Watermen appointed by the Rulers, are to carry Passengers cross the River on *Sundays*; and being paid for their Labour, the Overplus Money is to be apply'd to poor decayed Watermen, *etc.* And where Persons Travel on a *Sunday* with Boats, they are to be allow'd by a Justice of Peace, on Pain of forfeiting 5s. for every Offence. *Stat. 11 & 12 W.3.*

By the Stat. *4 & 5 Ann. c.13.* The Orders made for restraining Watermen free of the Company from taking Apprentices are declared void. And by this Act, on Notice of the Commissioners of the Admiralty, Watermen are to appear before the Company, to be sent on Board the Fleet: Not appearing they shall be imprisoned one Month, and be disabled for two Years.

No Waterman on the *Thames* shall take an Apprentice or Servant, unless he be an House-keeper, or have some known Habitation, and shall Register the same with the Clerk of the Company, on Pain of £10. And Apprentices are not to take upon them the Care of any Boat 'till 16 Years of Age, *etc.* except they have work'd with some able Waterman for two Years at least, under the Penalty of 10s. by Stat. *2 Geo.2. c.26.*

If any Person not having served Seven Years to a Waterman, *etc.* row any Boat on the said River for Hire, he shall forfeit £10 to be levied by Distress; and for want of sufficient Distress, the Lord Mayor of *London*, or any Justice for the Place where the Offence is commmitted, may by Warrant, commit the Offender to the House of Correction, not exceeding one Month, nor less than fourteen Days. *Stat. Ibid.*

But Gardeners Boats, Dung-Boats, Fishermen, Mill-Boats, Wood-Lighters, Western Barges, *etc.* are excepted, and may be rowed by Persons in such Manner as accustom'd.

All Constables, *etc.* are to be aiding and assisting in the Execution of this Act.

Rates of Watermen in and about London *and* Westminster.

	Oars	Sk
	s. d.	d.
From *London Bridge* to *Limehouse, New Lane,Shadwel-Dock, Bell-Wharf, Ratcliff-cros.s*	1 0	6
To *Wapping-Dock, Wapping New and Old Stairs, the Hermitage, Rotherhith* Church Stairs.	6	3
From St. *Olaves* to *Rotherhith* Church Stairs.	6	3
From *Billingsgate* and St. *Olaves* to St. *Saviour's Mill.*	6	3
All the Stairs between *London-Bridge* and *Westminster.*	6	3
From either Side from *London-Bridge* to *Lambeth* and *Vauxhall.*	1 0	6
From *Temple, Dorset,* and *Black Fryars* Stairs, or *Paul's Wharf,* to *Lambeth.*	8	4
From *Whitehall* to *Lambeth* and *Vauxhall.*	6	3
Over the Water directly between *Vauxhall* and *Limehouse.*	4	2

Distant from London, *etc. Rates of Oars.*

	Whole Fare	Company
	s. d.	s. d.
From *London* to *Gravesend.*	04 6	0 9
- *Woolwich*	02 6	0 4
- *Blackwall*	02 0	0 4
- *Greenwich* or *Deptford*	01 6	0 3
- *Chelsea, Battersea, Wandsworth*	01 6	0 3
- *Putney, Fulham, Barn Elms*	02 0	0 4
- *Hammersmith, Chiswick, Mortlake*	02 6	0 6
- *Brentford, Isleworth, Richmond*	03 6	0 6
- *Twittenham*	04 0	0 6
- *Kingston*	05 0	0 9
- *Hampton-Court*	06 0	1 0

- *Hampton-Town, Sunbury* and *Walton*	07 0	1 0
- *Weybridge* and *Chertsey*	10 0	1 0
- *Staines*	12 0	1 0
- *Windsor*	14 0	1 0

Hire of the Tilt down to *Gravesend* 22s. 6d.

Every single Person in the ordinary Passage 6d.

These Rates are set forth and appointed by the Lord Mayor and Aldermen, by Virtue of the first Statute afore mentioned.

ADDENDA

The Office of Constables.

Written by

SIR FRANCIS BACON, Kt.

To the first, *Of the Original of the Authority of Constables*, it may be said, *Caput inter nubila condit*, for the Authority was grounded upon the ancient Laws and Customs of this Kingdom, practised long before the Conquest, and intended and instituted for the Conservation of the Peace, and Repressing of all Manner of Disturbance, and Hurt of the People, and that as well by Way of Prevention, as Punishment; but yet so as they had no judicial Power to hear and determine any Cause, but only a ministerial Power; (as in the Answer to the 7th Article more at large is set down.)

As for the Office of the *High Constable*, the Original of that is yet more obscure: For though the High Constable's Authority and Jurisdiction hath the more ample Circuit, he being over the Hundred, and the Petty Constable over the Vill; yet I do not find the Petty Constable is subordinate to the High Constable, to be ordered by him: And therefore I doubt the High Constable was not *ab Origine*, but that when the Business of the Country increased, the Authority of the Justices of Peace was inlarged by divers Statutes: Then, for Convenience's Sake, the Office of High Constable grew in Use, for the Receiving of the Commands and Precepts from the Justices of Peace, and the Distributing of them to the Petty Constables: And in Token of this, the Election of the High Constables in most Parts of the Kingdom is by the Appointment of the Justices of Peace; whereas the Election of the Petty Constable is by the People. But there are two Things unto which the Office of Constables hath special Reference, and which of Necessity, or at least a Kind of Congruity, must precede the Jurisdiction of that Office: I mean, either the Things themselves, or somewhat that hath Similitude or Analogy towards them.

1. The one is the Division of the Territory or Gross of the Shires into Hundreds, Vills, and Towns: For the High Constable is Officer over the Hundred, and the Petty Constable over the Town or Vill.

2. The other is the Court-Leet, unto which the Constable is a proper Attendant and Minister: For there the Constables are chosen by the Jury, there they are sworn,

and there that Part of their Office which concerneth Information, is principally to be performed; for the Jury is to present Offences, and the Offenders; and are chiefly to take Light from the Constables of Matter of Disturbance, and Nusance of the Peace, which they in Respect of that Office are presumed to have best and most particular Knowledge of.

Now the Institution of the Leet is to three Ends.

1. The first, To take the ancient Oath of Allegiance of all Males above the Age of 12 Years.

2. The second, To enquire of all Offences against the Crown and Peace, and not to enquire only, and certify to the Justices of Gaol-Delivery; but those that are against the Peace simply, they are to enquire of and punish.

3. The third, Is to enquire of, punish and remove all publick Nusances concerning Infection of Air, Corruption of Victuals, Ease of Chaffer, and Contract of all other Things that may hurt or grieve the People in general in their Health, Quiet, and Welfare.

And to these three Ends, as Matters of Policy subordinate, the Court-Leet hath Power to call upon the Pledges that are to be taken of the Good Behaviour of the Resiants that are not Tenants, and to enquire of all Defaults of Officers, as Constables, Ale-Tasters, and the like; and likewise for the Choice of Constables, (as was said.)

1. The Jurisdiction of these Leets is either remaining in the King, and in that Case exercised by the Sheriff in his Turn, which is the Grand Leet granted over to Subjects, but yet is still the King's Court.

2. To the second, The Election (as was said of the Petty Constable) is at the Court-Leet by the Inquest that makes the Presentments: The Election of the Head Constables is by the Justices of the Peace at their Quarter-Sessions.

3. To the third, The Office of the Constable is annual, except they be removed.

4. To the fourth, They be Men (as is now used) of inferior, yea, of base Condition, which is a meer Abuse, or degenerating from the first Institution: For the Petty Constables in Towns ought to be of the better Sort of Resiants in the said Town, save that they ought not to be aged or sickly Men, but Men of able Bodies in Respect of the keeping Watch, and Toil of their Places.

Neither ought they to be in any Man's Livery. And the High Constables ought to be of the ablest of Freeholders, and of the most substantial Sort of Yeomen, next to the Degree of Gentlemen: But they ought to be such as are not incumbered with any other Office, as Mayor of the Town, Under-Sheriff, Bailiff, *etc.*

5. To the fifth, They have no Allowance, but are bound by Duty to perform their Office *gratis*, which may the rather be endured, because it is but annual, and likewise because they are not tied to keep or maintain any Servants, or Under-Ministers: For that everyone of the King's People within their Limits are bound to assist them.

6. To the sixth, Upon Complaint made of his Refusal to any one Justice of Peace, the said Justice may bind him over to the Sessions, where (if he cannot excuse himself by some Allegation that is just) he may be fined and imprisoned for his Contempt.

7. To the seventh, The Authority of the Constables, as it is substantive, and of it self, and astricted to the Warrants and Commands of the Justices of Peace; so again, it is original or additional: For either it was given them by the Common Law: or else annex'd by divers Statutes: And as for subordinate Power, wherein the Constable is only to execute the Commandment of the Justices of Peace, and likewise the additional Power which is given by divers Statutes, it is hard to comprehend them in any Brevity; for that they do correspond to the Office and Authority of the Justices of Peace, which is very large, and are created by the Branches of several Statutes, which are Things of divers and dispersed Natures. But for the Original and Substantive Power of a Constable, it may be reduced to three Heads:

1. For Matter of Peace only.
2. For Matters of Peace and the Crown.
3. For Matters of Nusance and Disorder, althoough they be not
   accompanied with Violence or Breach of Peace.

For pacifying of Quarrels begun, the Constables may, upon hot Words given, or Likelihood of Breach of Peace to ensue, command them, in the King's Name, to keep the Peace, and to depart and forbear; and so he may, where an Affray is made, part the same, and keep the Parties asunder, and arrest and commit the Breakers of the Peace, if they will not obey, and call Power to assist him for the same Purpose.

For Punishment of Breach of the Peace past, the Law is very sparing in giving any Power or Authority to Constables, because he hath no Power judicial; and the Use of his Office is rather for preventing or staying Mischief, than for punishing of Offences: For, in that Part he is rather to execute the Warrants of the Justices; or when sudden Matter ariseth upon his View, or notorious Circumstances, to apprehend the Offenders, and carry them before the Justices of Peace, and generally to imprison in like Cases of Necessity, where the Cause will not endure the present Carrying of the Party before the Justices. - And thus much for Matter of the Peace.

For Matters of the Crown, the Office of the Constable consists chiefly of four Parts, (viz.)

1. Arrest.
2. A Search.
3. Hue and Cry.
4. Seizure of Goods.

All which the Constable may perform of his own Authority, without any Warrant of the Justices of Peace. For,

1. First, If any Man will lay Murder or Felony to another's Charge, or do suspect him of Murder or Felony, he may declare it to the Constable; and the Constable ought, upon such Declaration or Complaint, to carry him before the Justice: And if by common Voice or Fame any Man be suspected, the Constable of Duty ought to arrest him, and bring him before a Justice, tho' there be no Accusation or Declaration.

2. Secondly, If any House be suspected for the Receiving or Harbouring of any Felon, the Constable, upon Complaint or common Fame, may search.

3. Thirdly, If any fly upon the Felony, the Constable ought to raise Hue and Cry.

4. Fourthly, The Constable ought to seize Goods, and keep them safe without impairing, and inventory them in the Presence of honest Neighbours. For Matter of Common Nusance of corrupting Air, Water or Victuals, or stopping or staightning or endangering any Passage, or general Deceits in Weights, Measures, Sizes, or counterfeiting of Wares and Things vendible: The Office of the Constable is to give (as much as in him is) Information of them, and of the Offenders in Leets, that they may be presented.

But because Leets are kept twice in the Year, and many of those Things require a speedy or present Remedy, the Constable in Things notorious, and of vulgar Nature, ought to forbid and repress them in the mean Time.

8. To the eighth, They are for their Contempt to be fined, or imprisoned, or both, by the Justices in their Sessions.

The Oath of Constables.

9. To the ninth, The Oath they take, is in this Manner; 'You shall swear, that you shall well and truly serve the King, and the Lord of the Law-Day: And you shall cause that the Peace of our Sovereign Lord the King shall be well and duly kept to your Power.

And you shall arrest all those that you see committing Riots, Debates and Affrays in Breach of the Peace.

And you shall well and duly endeavour your self to your best Knowledge, that the Statutes of *Wincester*, for Watch and Hue Cry, be put in Force; and the Statute made for the Punishment of sturdy Beggars, Vagabonds, Rogues, and other idle Persons, coming within your Office, that the Offenders be punished.

And you shall endeavour, upon Complaint made, to apprehend Barretors, and Riotous Persons making Affrays, and likewise to apprehend Felons: And if any of them make Resistance with Force and Multitude of Misdoers, you shall make Outcry, and pursue them 'till they be taken.

And you shall look unto such Persons as use unlawful Games.

And you shall have Regard unto the Maintenance of Artillery.

And you shall well and 'duly execute all Process and Precepts sent unto you from the Justices of Peace of the County.

And you shall make good and faithful Presentments of all Bloodsheds, Outcries, Affrays, and Rescues made within your Office.

And you shall well and duly, according to your Power and Knowledge, do that which belongeth to your Office of a Constable to do for this Year come.'

So help you God.

10. To the tenth, Their Authority is the same in Substance, differing only in the Extent: The Petty Constable serving only for one Town, Parish or Borough; the Head Constable serving for a whole Hundred: Neither is the Petty Constable subordinate to the Head Constable for any Commandment that proceeds from his own Authority. But it is used that the Precepts of the Justices be delivered unto the High Constables, who being few in Number, may better attend the Justices: And then the Head Constable, by Virtue thereof, makes his Precepts over to the Petty Constables.

The Compleat Parish Officer - Addenda.

11. To the eleventh, the Constable, in Case of Necessity, may appoint a Deputy, or in Default thereof, the Steward of the Leet may; which Deputy ought to be sworn before the said Steward.

The Office of Constables consists wholly in these three Things, viz.

1. Their Office concerning the Conservation of the Peace.
2. The serving of the Precepts and Warrants of the Justices.
3. Their Attendance for the Execution of the Statutes.

The Office of Constables is of great Power and Authority, especially by Night, at which Time they have the whole Rule and Government, and ought to be obeyed, as well without their Staff of Office or Authority, as with it; provided they declare and make themselves known by that Title, and in the King's Majesty's Name: For it is not the Staff which makes the Constable, but the Office which he is sworn unto: And therefore he may command, in his Majesty's Name, any Person or Persons to go along with and aid and assist him, in and upon all Occasions: For while his Majesty and his Ministers of Quality take their Rest in the Night, the Constable's Office is to be intrusted with that Part of the City or Precinct unto which he is called, for fear of Uproars and Robberies, and such like Outrages: And for that Reason Constables ought to be cherished and respected, if they faithfully discharge that Trust committed to them. And let them that are chosen into this Office be both faithful and trusty to discharge the Trust which is committed unto them. And let not future Hope, nor present Reward blind their Eyes, nor make deaf their Ears, lest some Danger may ensue, which may prove their Ruin and Destruction.

Felix quem faciunt aliena pericula Cautum.

FINIS.

Notes about the Author.

The British Library holds five editions of The Compleat Parish Officer, though not this particular edition. The author signs these with either a G. or G.J. and is presumed to be Giles Jacob who was born in 1686 at Romsey, Hampshire, a son of a malster. He died on 8 May 1744.

He was a prolific compiler and published amongst others "The Compleat Court-keeper, or Land-Steward's Assistant" 1713; "The Country Gentleman's Vade Mecum, containing an Account of the best Methods to improve Lands" 1717; "The Compleat Sportsman" 1718; "The Laws of Appeal and Murder" 1719; "The Laws of Taxation" 1720;"The Land Purchaser's Companion" 1720; "The Common Law common-placed" 1726; "City Liberties" 1732.

The editions of The Compleat Parish Officer which are held by the British Library are:- 5th Edition 1729; 6th Edition 1731; 8th Edition 1738; 9th Edition 1741; 10th Edition 1744.

References taken from Mozley and Whiteley's Law Dictionary

Bulstr.	Bulstrode	1610-1626	King's Bench
Calthr.	Calthrop's Cases on the Customs of London	1609-1618	King's Bench
Co. Rep.	Coke, Sir Edward	1572-1616	Common Law
Cro. Eliz.	Croke, time of Elizabeth	1582-1603	Common Law
Dalt.	Dalton's Justice		
Dyer		1513-1581	Common Law
Godb.	Goldbolt	1574-1637	Queen's or Kong's Bench
Het.	Hetley	1627-1631	Common Pleas
T. Jones's Rep.	Jones Sir T.	1667-1685	Common Law
Keb.	Keble	1661-1677	King's Bench
Latch. Rep.		1625-1628	King's Bench
Leo.	Leonard	1552-1615	Common Law
Lev.	Levinz	1660-1696	Common Law
Litt.	Littleton	1627-1631	Common Pleas and Exch.
Lutw.	Lutwyche	1682-1704	Common Pleas
Mar.	March's New Cases	1639-1642	Common Law
Mod.	Modern Reports (Leach's)	1669-1755	All the Courts
Noy	Noy	1558-1649	Common Law
Owen	Owen	1557-1614	Common Law
Palm.	Palmer	1619-1629	King's Bench

Plow.	Plowden	1550-1580	Common Law
Poph.	Popham	1591-1627	Common Law
Raym.	Raymond Sir T.	1660-1683	Common Law
Rayn.	Rayner's Tithe Cases	1575-1782	All the Courts
Roll. Rep.	Rolle Sir H.	1614-1625	King's Bench
Salk. Rep.	Salkeld	1689-1712	King's Bench (principally)
Saund.	Saunders	1666-1672	King's Bench
Sid.	Siderfin	1657-1670	King's Bench
Skin.	Skinner	1681-1697	King's Bench
Sty.	Style	1646-1655	King's or Upper Bench
Vent.	Ventris	1668-1691	All the Courts